EXPLSIVE
INHERITANCE

Matthew Jones

ISBN 978-1-0980-9151-4 (paperback)
ISBN 978-1-0980-9152-1 (digital)

Christian Faith Publishing, Inc.
832 Park Avenue
Meadville, PA 16335
www.christianfaithpublishing.com

Printed in the United States of America

His divine power has granted to us everything
pertaining to life and godliness,
through the true knowledge of Him who called
us by His own glory and excellence.
For by these things He has granted to us His
precious and magnificent promises,
so that by them you may become partakers of the divine nature,
having escape the corruption that is in the world by lust.

—2 Peter 1:3–4

CONTENTS

Dunamis/Dynamis (doo-nam-is)

Strong's Concordance: Greek: 1411
(miraculous) power, might, strength, force, ability, efficacy,
energy, powerful deeds, deeds showing
physical power, marvelous works.

(from 1410/dynamai, "able, having ability")
properly, "ability to perform";
for the believer, power to achieve by applying
the Lord's inherent abilities.
"Power through God's ability."

1411 (dynamis) used 120 times in the New Testament.

PREFACE

Explosive Inheritance is a book written from a place of desperation, a desperation driven by the desire for people to understand the power and purpose of the real Christian life. Forget what you've heard. Christianity is not about going to church, attending a Bible study, reading an old book, or saying scripted premeal prayers. No! The real Christian life is one empowered by God to fulfill the purpose of God, namely to save the world.

As a culture, we have become obsessed with stories of superheroes while remaining blind to the fact that Jesus paid for us to receive an inheritance of power and purpose that far surpasses any superhero.

For too long, people have been taught that their God-given inheritance is waiting for them in heaven. While that is true, God also has an inheritance for you right here, right now.

Your *Explosive Inheritance* is ready. Are you?

ACKNOWLEDGMENTS

For my God and Savior, thank you for your grace. Without you, I am nothing, have nothing, and can do nothing. YHWH, you are my everything. Eternally, thank you.

For my wife, Alissa, who has been my constant companion along this journey. Thank you for always believing in me and encouraging me to trust Jesus. Thank you for graciously and patiently pushing me to pursue God's presence. Thank you for sacrificially serving our family. Without you, this book wouldn't have happened. I am forever grateful for you, my best friend.

For my daughter Ellie, I adore you and look forward to the day that we continue this legacy of following and leading others to the Lord Jesus Christ together. I love you unconditionally and am proud to be your dad.

For anyone who believes that following Jesus is boring. For anyone who longs for more in life. For anyone looking for purpose and the ability to accomplish their calling, this *Explosive Inheritance* is for you.

INTRODUCTION

As a kid, I grew up collecting comic cards.

For those who don't speak nerd, these were trading cards with comic characters on them.

Superheroes specifically.

I had boxes upon boxes of them. Marvel, DC, it didn't matter, I loved them all. I even had a special collection that I kept in a blue binder. This binder was full of my most sacred cards. Cards that were set apart for my personal enjoyment. Cards that were not for sale. Cards I wouldn't think of trading. These were cards that would be worth something someday, but I didn't care. They were mine.

As I flipped through the pages of these coveted characters, I would sometimes daydream about what it would be like to inherit their powers.

I dreamt about flying like Superman, shooting laser beams from my face like Cyclops, swinging from webs like Spider-Man, and having monstrous muscles and superhuman strength like the Hulk.

Don't act like I'm the only one...

If you could be any superhero or have any superpower, which would you choose? It's a common question.

Me personally, I would pick Spider-Man. Why? Spider-Man has the most realistic story. It presents the possibility of actually happening. Check this out.

It's highly unlikely that anyone is actually born a demigod or mutant, so Thor and all the X-Men are out.

It's highly unlikely to be born into a family of billionaires, be bitten by a flying rodent, and become the next Batman.

It's highly unlikely that the government is going to runs tests on you turning you into a super soldier like Captain America.

But it is possible, at least in my mind, that a normal person could be bitten by a spider that happened to be exposed to radioactive chemicals.

It's at least possible.

If you're going to become a superhero, this is your best shot.

My wife will push back and say that Batman is more realistic, but I honestly don't consider Batman a superhero. I mean the guy literally doesn't have a single superpower other than being rich.

Right?

What would have happened to Bruce Wayne without all that money?

Would Bruce Wayne have ever become Batman if he wasn't a billionaire?

No.

He would have just been a regular boy with no parents who got bit by a bat. End of story.

Maybe he becomes Bruce Blart, Gotham City mall cop, but he doesn't become Batman.

As you can see, I've thought about this a time or two. In fact, it was a road trip favorite. The superhero question has provided hours of entertainment on drives to Yosemite National Park, Southern California, and Lake Tahoe. My favorite was when the superhero question eventually evolved into a game of "Would you rather..."

Would you rather have the power to fly or the ability to see through walls? Know the future or change the past? Shoot spaghetti from your armpits or have bad breath that could paralyze your opponent?

The questions only got weirder from there.

Anyway, as I grew older, the questions quieted, dreams of becoming a superhero began to fade, and my blue binder started collecting dust in the closet.

Where did this obsession with the supernatural come from anyway?

From superheroes to *Harry Potter*, Disney to the *Walking Dead*, *The Twilight Zone* to *Twilight*, it seems that everywhere we look, in our movies, TV shows, books, and comics, our entertainment is covered with stories, characters, and series about the supernatural.

As it turns out, there is a reason we are drawn to these possibilities.

The reason hunger exists is because food exists. The reason thirst exists is because water exists. The reason exhaustion exists is because sleep exists. For every appetite, there is something available to satisfy that desire. The same is true for the supernatural: the desire exists because something exists to satiate it. Little did I know at the time, but I was about to find out what that something was.

What began as a boyhood fantasy, the desire to become a superhero, would soon take on a whole new reality in college when I read the historical accounts about Jesus of Nazareth.

Let me back up.

When I first read the Bible in college, I had already experienced an encounter with the Author. Yes, I'm talking about God. We had recently met. I'll share more about that in a moment. But that was my only motivation. Why else would a college frat boy pick up a Bible instead of a beer?

Anyway, a few days before embarking on my biblical adventure, my life was on the highway to hell. It's true. I was pursuing a life in complete opposition to God. All I cared about at this time was getting laid, getting paid, drinking, doing drugs, and partying as hard as humanly possible. I didn't care about God, church, religion, my family, or my future. I was living for the now with no concern for the consequences. But right before Christmas vacation during my senior year in college, I overdosed on drugs and had a near-death experience that led to an encounter with the God of the Bible.

In an audible voice, God told me that he loved me, despite my disobedience. God then confronted my life of rebellion and revealed the consequences that would inevitably come if I continued to reject him. Then, in a most unexpected twist of events, he invited me to follow him. God told me that he had already paid the price for my sin, cleared my spiritual debt, and set me free when he was crucified on Calvary. All I had to do was place my faith in what Jesus did and trust that what he said was true. If I did that, he promised me a new start, a new life, and the ability rewrite my history with an adventure of biblical proportions.

That was the easiest decision of my life. I mean, what choice did I really have? Of course, there was a choice, but the options were limited and the alternative was unappealing at best.

When God speaks to you, when you encounter the God who created all things, and all doubt of his existence is removed, and you are confronted with the weight of his holiness and the consequences of sin, what else can you do but worship him?

So out of reverence, appreciation, awe, and wonder, I started to pursue a relationship with my Rescuer. I had no idea what I was doing, but I began with the Bible. I became a student of my Savior.

In my studies of scripture, to my surprise, I discovered that Jesus had done things that only superheroes could do. There were literally pages upon pages of eyewitness testimonies about Jesus healing the sick, opening blind eyes, unstopping deaf ears, delivering people from demons, confronting the devil, and even raising the dead.

Jesus not only claimed to be God, he walked around doing God things.

As I kept reading, I realized that Jesus also made many promises about an inheritance. Something about power from heaven. Power to heal, save, restore, destroy, rebuild, and the power to work miracles.

Superpowers.

More like supernatural powers.

Either way, Jesus promised to provide his people, his followers, those who believed in him, with the same power that he had.

If that wasn't enough, Jesus took the promise a step further. He said that his followers would not only be able to do the same things that he was doing, but even greater things (John 14:12).

But then, after three years of making these public promises, telling others about the kingdom of God and predicting his death and resurrection, it happened.

Everything that Jesus said would happen, did.

He was crucified and killed. He resurrected from the dead on the third day. Jesus then revealed himself to over four hundred people over a period of forty days before disappearing into the clouds like Superman.

Jesus predicted all of it. Not a single promise went unfulfilled.

If Jesus truly knew the future and fulfilled what he promised through his death, burial, and resurrection, could his other promises be true as well?

What about the inheritance?

Could the promise to empower his people with supernatural, God-like capabilities be possible?

As I finished the gospel accounts of Jesus and flipped to the next section of scripture called the book of Acts. I read that after the Resurrection, Jesus instructed his disciples to wait in Jerusalem for the power he promised. His followers did as they were told and waited a total of ten days.

On the tenth day, their inheritance arrived as promised. It came with the sound of a violent rushing wind and fire from heaven that filled the room where they were waiting. As a result, just like Jesus had promised, his followers were filled with supernaturally explosive power.

From that moment forward, we see the disciples doing the same supernatural stuff that Jesus did during his ministry. They not only told the story of what Jesus said and did, they demonstrated what they had inherited and extended the invitation for others to receive the inheritance as well.

The result?

Today, two thousand years later, we are still talking about Jesus, the acts of the disciples, and the power that God gifted as an inheritance. In fact, there are literally billions of people around the planet, on every continent, country, state, county, and city, that have encountered this Jesus, received his inheritance, and have the power to do God things like Jesus did.

After reading the Jesus story, researching the historical veracity of the biblical testimonies, and personally encountering the God of the Bible, I too have become one of those people empowered with the promised inheritance.

My purpose in writing this book is to extend the same invitation for you to receive yours. And if you have already received Jesus Christ as your Lord and Savior, this book is designed to show you how to invest the inheritance you have, whether you knew about your inheritance or not.

The truth is, following Jesus Christ and becoming a Christian is more than going to a building on Sundays or reading a book. Following Jesus is not about becoming a good person and doing good things, although you will. Following Jesus is about becoming more like God and doing God things, supernatural things, superhero things, the same things that Jesus did and more.

To become a Christian is literally to become a little Christ. No, I'm not talking about Will Ferrell's eight-pound six-ounce baby Jesus; I'm talking about water-into-wine, walking-on-water, sword-wielding, table-flipping, demon-stomping, death-defeating, heaven-inhabiting King of kings and Lord of lords, Jesus.

And the same power that raised Jesus from the dead is the same power available as your inheritance.

As you open the following pages, I am going to show you what God's word says about your inheritance, how to receive it, and, ultimately, what to do with it.

CHAPTER 1

You Have an Inheritance

Imagine with me for a moment that you have just attended the funeral of your father.

You loved your dad and will miss him greatly. You also have the peace of knowing that he loved you too.

After the funeral comes the reception. You shake hands, receive hugs, and hear countless condolences from family and friends.

The next day you gather together again to hear the reading of your father's will.

He left the estate to your mom, baseball card collection to your brother, and some objects of sentimental value to your sister.

Wondering if your father forgot to leave you anything, you notice a small rectangular box sitting on the attorney's desk.

"What's in the box?" you inquire.

"This box?" says the lawyer, pointing to the item representing the only hope you have of receiving an inheritance.

"Yes, the only box on your desk. Who is it for?"

The lawyer opens an envelope and reads your name. "It's for you."

After receiving the box, you notice a letter taped to the bottom:

> *My dearest son, out of everything I owned, this box*
> *contains my most prized possession.*
> *I want you to have it.*

Remember me, my legacy, what I did; and you will know what to do.

I love you,
Dad

Wiping a tear from the corner of your eye, you open the box to discover...

A stick of dynamite?

Why would your dad leave you dynamite?

You reflect on your father's final words, trying to figure it out: *"Remember me, my legacy, what I did; and you will know what to do."*

Your dad owned a construction company. He was in the building business. He loved demolition days, but it was the magnificent structures that he built from the ground up that brought him the greatest joy.

Am I supposed to build something? Blow something up? Why would Dad leave me dynamite?

These are the same questions I had when discovering that God also left us dynamite as our inheritance.

Yes.

Dynamite.

Every time God's word describes the power that Jesus promised as our inheritance, we see the Greek word *dunamis*, which is where we derive the English word *dynamite*.

The word *dunamis* actually appears over 120 times in the New Testament describing strength, power, or ability. But not just any power. The word refers to miraculous power or marvelous works, superpower, the ability to work supernatural signs and wonders. Dunamis is explosive dynamite power, and this power is the gift of God.

In Acts 1:8 Jesus tells his followers, "You shall receive power when the Holy Spirit comes upon you, and you shall be my witnesses in Jerusalem, in all Judea, and Samaria, and to the ends of the earth."

Jesus said we will receive dunamis or dynamite power through the Holy Spirit.

One thing that I love about Jesus is his leadership style. Jesus practiced what he preached. He never tells us to do anything that he hasn't already demonstrated himself.

If Jesus said it, he has already done it.

For instance, when Jesus was baptized, the Holy Spirit descended from heaven in the form of a dove and remained on him. Before that moment, not a single miracle had been recorded about Jesus's ministry. After his baptism, Jesus was not only full of the Holy Spirit, he left the desert empowered by the Holy Spirit, and according to scripture, "There are not enough books in the world to contain all that Jesus did" (John 21:25).

Jesus promised that we will receive dunamis power when the Holy Spirit comes upon us, and he demonstrated that truth at the start of his public ministry.

So if the explosive power of our inheritance comes with the Holy Spirit, we should probably explore a little more about this Holy Spirit.

Shall we?

CHAPTER 2

What Is the Inheritance?

God's word tells us that the Holy Spirit landed on Jesus like a dove. Does that mean it was similar to the spider that landed on Peter Parker?

Not quite.

The Holy Spirit is not a bird, a box of explosives, or any other object or animal. The Holy Spirit is also not a force of nature or super-nature like from Star Wars. Ultimately, the Holy Spirit is not a power but a person.

Let me say that differently. Your inheritance is not a "what" but a "who."

The inheritance is a person, and that person has dunamis power.

I'm not talking explosive power like a linebacker or bodybuilder, no. Think "big bang" type of power. The explosive power to speak all of creation into existence type of power. The type of power to tell the stars where to stand. The type of power to tell the sun how to shine and the planets when to rotate. The type of power to command the waters to stop at the sand. The type of power found only in the great I Am.

I am talking about God.

Your inheritance is God.

The gift is God dwelling with us, his people, his creation (Lam. 3:24; Ps. 16:5).

According to the Bible, God has a long history of living with his people:

In the Garden of Eden, where God planted the first people, Adam and Eve, God dwelt with two.

When God established the Tabernacle and Temple, he dwelt with a few.

Through Jesus, aka Immanuel, aka "God with us," God dwelt with many.

Then through the Holy Spirit, God could dwell with any.

But how can you inherit a person?

The priests of the Old Testament know a thing or two about this, so let's check in with the Levites.

Inherited Employment

Descendants of Aaron, the brother of Moses, the Levites were one of the twelve tribes of Israel. By profession, the Levites were the priests of the Lord. Among other duties, it was in their job description to offer the sacrifices that would temporarily cover the sins of Israel.

The Levites earned their esteemed priestly position through Aaron, who was willing to serve God when Moses wasn't. You see, Moses was chosen by God to set his people free from Pharaoh in Egypt, but Moses had a speech impediment, and he let that insecurity prevent him from fully trusting in the Lord to do what he had promised.

Instead, Aaron stepped in and was God's mouthpiece to Pharaoh since Moses had a stammer. Aaron was a servant to the Lord from the start, and God rewarded him and his descendants with the highly regarded position as priests.

After the Lord brought Israel out of slavery in Egypt, through the partnership of Moses and Aaron, God began to prepare his people for the Promised Land. He taught the people what total dependence on the Lord looked like as God faithfully provided for all of their needs in the desert. God also gave the Israelites a set of laws known as the Ten Commandments that would set his people apart from the other inhabitants in the Promised Land. These laws were intended to make his people different or countercultural to those already living in Canaan, the land promised to the people of Israel.

Not only did God want his people to be set apart from the surrounding nations, he wanted his priests to be separate from the rest of the people as well. Like the comic cards in my blue binder, the Levites, the priests of God, were his coveted collection that were set apart for God's personal enjoyment and purposes.

How does God demonstrate this favor?

All twelve tribes of Israel were assigned to receive a portion of the Promised Land, a land described as "flowing with milk and honey," as their inheritance. All tribes except the Levites.

That's right. The Levites were so special that they did not receive an inheritance of land. Instead, the Levites could only live in the land of their brothers while serving the Lord.

Before deciding that this is a raw deal, check out what the Lord said to Aaron about his inheritance: "Then the LORD said to Aaron, *'You shall have no inheritance in their land nor own any portion among them; I am your portion and your inheritance among the sons of Israel'*" (Num. 18:20).

Aaron's people would not be receiving the land; instead, they received the Landowner. They did not get the creation; they got the Creator.

To better understand the gravity of this gift, let's read a more comprehensive description of the Levite's inheritance: *"The Levitical priests, the whole tribe of Levi, shall have no portion or inheritance with Israel; they shall eat the Lord's offerings by fire and his portion. They shall have no inheritance among their countrymen; the Lord is the inheritance, as he promised them"* (Deut. 18:2).

One of God's commandments required the people of Israel to present the best portion of their land to the Lord as an offering. That meant the first and best portions of their produce, cattle, wine, grain, whatever the land produced, the best portion of the produce belonged to the Lord.

According to God, the Promised Land was the best, most beautiful, and most glorious piece of land on the planet (Ezek. 20:6). God reserves the absolute best for his people.

As an act of gratitude and thanksgiving, God's people were required to give the best produce from the best land back to the Lord as an offering or sacrifice.

And what was God going to do with those offerings?

Share them!

With whom?

You guessed it, the Levites.

Although they did not receive an inheritance of land, the Lord was their inheritance and with the Lord came the best of the best. Not only were the Israelites required to provide housing and land for the Levites to inhabit within their allotted inheritance, they were required to give the Levites the first fruits of their labor, the best food and drink the world had to offer.

To inherit God is to inherit the greatest gift known to humankind. There is nothing better.

You want to hear something super amazing?

God's Word calls all Christ followers a royal priesthood.

It's true!

But don't take my word for it. Here is the word of the Lord as penned by the Apostle Peter: *"You are a chosen people, a royal priesthood, a holy nation, God's special possession, that you may declare the praises of him who called you out of darkness into his wonderful light"* (1 Pet. 2:9).

Like the Levites, as followers of Jesus, we are priests.

Do you know what that means?

As priests, our inheritance is not the land on which we live, our inheritance is the Lord.

Our explosive inheritance is the presence and person of God.

Sure, God could give us an inheritance of land, money, power, prestige, and all the kingly things of the kingdom; but instead, God has chosen to give us something with infinitely more value, the King himself.

Like the Levites, if you inherit the King, you get the best of the kingdom as well, which, of course, includes the King's explosive dunamis power.

The King is with us.

25

That's the gift!

The Spirit of God, the Spirit of Christ, the Spirit of the Father, the Lord, aka the Holy Spirit, is the person of God living in you (Rom. 8:9; 1 Pet. 1:11; Gal. 4:6; 2 Cor. 3:17; 2 Sam. 23:2; Matt. 10:20).

Just as Jesus walked around with the Holy Spirit in him, we too, as followers of Christ, have the Holy Spirit, the presence and person of God dwelling in us.

When did this happen?

The moment you believed in Jesus, God's only begotten Son.

The Bible says it like this: *"When you believed, you were marked in him with a seal, the promised Holy Spirit, who is a deposit guaranteeing our inheritance until the redemption of those who are God's possession—to the praise of his glory"* (Eph. 1:14).

What does this mean?

If Jesus Christ is your Lord and Savior, you have an inheritance from the Father. It's a promise! Jesus said so himself: *"Behold, I am sending forth the promise from My Father upon you; but you are to stay in the city until you are clothed with power from heaven"* (Luke 24:49).

No one wants us to understand this more than the apostle Paul, who penned, *"I pray that you will understand the incredible greatness of God's power for us who believe him. This is the same mighty power that raised Christ from the dead and seated him in the place of honor at God's right hand in the heavenly realms"* (Eph. 1:19).

If all this Holy Spirit stuff is hard to understand, you're in good company. Thankfully, the apostle Paul, the author of many New Testament books, described this mystery plainly. He said the mystery that God has been keeping hidden for generations and is now disclosed to the Lord's people is this: Jesus lives in you! (Col. 1:26–27; Gal. 2:20).

Yes, through the Holy Spirit, Jesus Christ lives in you! It doesn't get any plainer than that.

If this is true, what would you do?

What would you do if the God of the Bible, the God who created the entire universe; the God who walked with Adam and Eve in the garden; the God who spoke to Abraham and led him to Canaan;

the God who warned Noah of the flood; the God who spoke to Moses in a burning bush and freed Israel from Egyptian slavery; the God who split the Red Sea; the God who protected and guided his people through the desert as a pillar of fire at night and a cloud covering during the day; the God who provided for his people with water from a rock and manna and quail from heaven; the God who helped David defeat Goliath; the God who delivered Israel from the enemies in the Promised Land; the God who broke down the walls of Jericho; the God who gave Solomon all of his wisdom; the God who spoke to the Old Testament prophets about the promised and coming Messiah; the God who left his throne in heaven to become a man in Jesus Christ; the God who healed the sick, raised the dead, delivered people from demons, lived a perfect life, died a sacrificial death, defeated sin, death, hell and the grave; the God who is alive today, sitting on the throne of heaven; the God who sent his Holy Spirit, his very presence, to dwell inside of you. What would you do, and how would you live if you truly believed that this God, the God of the Bible, lived in you?

Try to define impossible.

I mean, truly, what would be impossible for you at that point?

If God lives in you, what problem is too complex, what chain is too big to break, what mountain is too big to move, what lack couldn't be met, what soul couldn't be saved, what disease couldn't be demolished, what reason would we ever have to lose hope, what cliff is too high to climb, what could keep you from fulfilling your purpose?

Nothing.

The correct answer is nothing.

Like the Levites, with God as your inheritance, you have everything needed and you lack nothing.

As we continue to uncover the gift of God, the dunamis power that has been made available to all, through the Holy Spirit, I pray, like Paul, that God will give you the understanding and insight to comprehend the greatness of this inheritance.

Gifted Inheritance

In the last section, we discovered that with God as your inheritance you not only get God, you also get the gifts of God.

I personally love gifts. In fact, gift giving and receiving is one of my top love languages.

Michael Scott, a character from the TV show comedy *The Office*, said, "Presents are the best way to show someone how much you care. It's like this tangible thing that you can point to and say, 'Hey, man, I love you this many dollars' worth.'" Like Michael, I love to express my love, appreciation, and gratitude through gift giving.

Everything about the gift-giving process brings me joy. I love purchasing the present, picking the perfect wrapping paper, and, finally, presenting the gift to the person. There is something about seeing the expression on people's faces when they receive a gift that is truly life-giving. Jesus said it best: "It is better to give than to receive." But let's be real. I love receiving gifts too. That part never gets old.

For me, when it comes to receiving gifts, part of the excitement comes from the mystery of the packaging. Some of the greatest gifts I've ever received have come in the most unassuming packages. I've learned this lesson from my mom. She has turned gift giving into an art form. You never know what surprises my mom has hidden in the most obscure boxes.

Recently, for Christmas, my mom gave me a metal Skittles container. To be honest, I wasn't excited. I like to stay fit and didn't want to consume a bunch of candy that could potentially ruin the body I was building. Since I wasn't planning on eating the candy, I could have completely disregarded the gift assuming that I understood what was inside. I could have faked a smile, thanked my mom with a hug, and put that candy box on a shelf or cupboard in our kitchen. However, knowing my mom and the gift giver she is, I knew there was more than meets the eye. True to form, when I opened my mother's gift, I found that it was stuffed full of cash, not candy.

What would have happened if I never opened that box? What if I simply assumed that I knew what was inside?

Nothing. I would have never enjoyed the buying power of those bills. I may have even had needs or wants that my mom's money could have met, but without opening the box, I wouldn't have experienced any of the benefits.

Sadly, many Christians live like that today—unfulfilled, powerless, and spiritually impoverished while our explosive inheritance sits on the shelf collecting dust.

I wonder how many prayers haven't been answered because the solution was sitting in an unopened box.

Like my mom's generous gift, not all of God's gifts make sense based on the wrapping paper.

Did it make sense for God's presence to take the form of a bird? Not really. Thankfully, Jesus wasn't deterred by the packaging of the dove. Can you imagine him shoeing away the Holy Spirit. "Get out of here, pigeon! I've got God stuff to do!"

You see, God has given us an incredible inheritance through the Holy Spirit. The Holy Spirit has powerful gifts intended to not only meet our needs and desires, but the wants and needs of the world around us as well. However, it is possible to have the inheritance, to receive the Holy Spirit, without ever opening the packaging to tap into God's power and provision. Which is why we're going to open these gifts together to see what God has generously provided for his people.

God-Sized Gifts

The apostle Paul, in his letter to the church in Corinth, tells the congregation, "Now about the gifts of the Spirit, brothers and sisters, I do not want you to be uninformed" (1 Cor. 12:1). He then goes on to explain that the Holy Spirit has a great variety of gifts to give his people, but the Holy Spirit is the one who distributes them as he sees fit (1 Cor. 12:4,11; Heb. 2:4).

We'll get into the "why these gifts have been given" a bit later, but first, what gifts does Paul describe?

We are told about nine gifts of the Holy Spirit, which include wisdom, knowledge, faith, healing, miracles, prophecy, distinguishing between spirits, various types of tongues, and the interpretation of tongues (1 Cor. 12:8–10). I will later refer to this list of gifts as the power list because they are typically manifested in outwardly explosive ways.

Besides the power list, Paul also goes on to describe other gifts from God in his letter to the church in Rome and Ephesus as well. These gifts are equally important and include the apostle, prophet, evangelist, pastor and teacher along with the gifts of service, teaching, exhortation, generosity, leadership, mercy, helping, and guidance (Rom. 12:6–8; 1 Cor. 12:28–30, Eph. 4:11).

Throughout this book, I will be sharing examples of these gifts from my experiences, but before I do, it is vitally important to understand what these gifts are and what they are not.

What Money Cannot Buy

When Paul describes the gifts of the Spirit in 1 Corinthians 12–14, he uses the word *charismata*.

Are you ready for a linguistics lesson?

The Greek root *charis* means "grace, unmerited favor, or goodwill that is undeserved." Taking our Greek study, a step further, the word *charisma* is translated in the New Testament as "gift" and when made plural, the Greek word *charismata* means "free undeserved gifts or grace gifts."

Why is this important?

The gifts of the Holy Spirit are not merit badges for good behavior. They cannot be bought or earned. God's gifts are given by his grace through the Holy Spirit, not rewarded through our works. Also, the purpose of these power gifts is to glorify God and his grace. They should always point back to God and are purposed to give him glory.

Some pridefully see spiritual gifts as a status symbol, but we will soon discover that the gifts are meant for service, not status.

Now, as I mentioned earlier, the apostle Paul is describing and explaining God's gifts to various churches. The church who happened to receive the list of power gifts came from Corinth. Let me share a little context about Corinth.

The city of Corinth was basically modern-day Las Vegas, a place where people went to party, conduct business, and enjoy prostitution. Was Corinth a religious location? Depends how you define religious. You see, the Corinthians worshiped Aphrodite, the goddess of licentious love and promiscuous sexual behavior. The temple of Aphrodite actually included a thousand professional prostitutes where people came to worship through sexual sacrifices. Corinth was essentially a place of pagan revelry without regulations regarding morality. If it felt good, it was god. Those were the rules of Corinth.

Speaking of God, he loved the people who inhabited the sinful city of Corinth so much that he had the apostle Paul plant a church there. However, it didn't take long for Paul to receive reports that the people in the church were allowing Aphrodite worship and the ways of Corinth to infiltrate the church. In Paul's letter to the Corinthian church, he calls them worldly. Why? Because they looked more like the Corinthian culture than like Christ. Paul also addressed them as babies in the faith, infants who were only mature enough to handle milk instead of solid food.

Ouch, Paul.

However, these criticisms were apparently warranted as the people attending the Corinthian church were getting drunk on communion wine, suing each other in court, and even had cases of sexual immorality that you would only see on *Jerry Springer*. I'm talking about people having sex with their own parents! This was one jacked-up church!

Despite all of their disgusting behavior, this did not stop the Holy Spirit from giving his supernatural gifts. In fact, the Corinthian church was overflowing with miracles, signs, and wonders. The Holy Spirit was manifesting his gifts so much that Paul had to write a training manual on how to handle the power appropriately.

The Corinthian church is meant to encourage us to seek God, who gives gifts to his people based on his grace, not our goodness.

Speaking of seeking God for the gifts, Paul instructed the church to eagerly seek the greater gifts. It may seem strange that God would have a hierarchy of the gifts he gives, but Paul literally puts them in order starting with apostle, prophet, teacher, miracles, healing, helping, guidance, and tongues. Paul then says that he would love for everyone to speak in tongues, but that it is better to prophesy.

So look at the list of gifts again, and ask God for the ones you want. Ultimately, it is up to the Holy Spirit to discern if and when each gift is given, but it doesn't hurt to ask.

Now at this point, some of you may be thinking, *Okay, I get it. The Holy Spirit is our inheritance, and he gives awesome gifts. So how do we actually receive our inheritance?*

That, my friends, is a great question, one that only Spider-Man can answer.

CHAPTER 3

How to Receive Your Inheritance

I began this book tempting you with the possibility of becoming as powerful, impactful, and purposeful as your favorite superhero. In the next chapter, you will discover the practical process to make that fantasy a reality.

So let me ask you, what do Spider-Man and the Holy Spirit have in common?

More than most would ever dare to compare.

As it turns out, the same process that turned a normal high school student named Peter Parker into the web-slinging superhero is the same process required to receive your inheritance.

I call it the Peter Parker Process.

I've made it easy to learn and easy to remember. In fact, there are only four phases, and lucky for you, they all start with the same letter.

Just as there are four *E*s in the name "P*e*ter Park*e*r Proc*e*ss," there are four phases that all start with the letter, you guessed it, *E*.

The four phases of the Peter Parker Process are as follows:

1. Encounter
2. Empower
3. Exercise
4. Employ

That shouldn't make any sense at the moment, but as we take a step into the life of Spider-Man, it will.

Before Peter Parker became a superhero, he had an **encounter** with a radioactive spider.

As Peter Parker began to transform from the spider bite, he discovered that his encounter came with new powers, abilities, and tools.

Transitioning to the **empower** phase, Peter Parker found that his hands could now stick to anything he touched. He could scale walls, crawl on ceilings, shoot webs from his wrists; and he even developed "spidey senses" that tingled when trouble was near.

After being empowered, Peter Parker then entered the **exercise** phase. This is where Peter began to practice his new skills and work on mastering the new tools, power, and equipment he inherited.

In this phase, we see Peter trying to swing from trees, jump from rooftops, and work on aiming his webs. And Peter Parker wasn't perfect; he failed often. But as Master Yoda once said, "The greatest teacher, failure is."

Now that Peter Parker has had an encounter, been empowered, and exercised his inheritance, he swings into the final phase of the process called **employ**.

The employ phase is where Peter Parker finally embraces not only his new identity, but also his purpose. This is the phase where Peter Parker takes his new tools and his training and starts to pursue his purpose, using his power to save and protect the people around him.

This is also the phase where Peter Parker takes ownership of his uncle Ben's wise words that "with great power comes great responsibility."

Peter Parker was no longer a normal high school student.

No longer could Peter Parker be consumed or controlled by the cares of high school life, social media, skateboarding, or sports.

Peter Parker was transformed by a process and empowered for a purpose.

Peter Parker was now Spider-Man, and his life would never be the same.

There you have it—four simple stages, one powerful process. So let's get practical.

To understand the Peter Parker Process from a biblical perspective, we are now going to look at the life of the apostle Paul who also experienced this process and walked away with more than just webs. Instead, when Paul was finished with the process, he was transformed into a Holy-Spirit-inhabited, Jesus-preaching, disciple-making, miracle-working, world-changing, Bible-book-writing, death-defying, church-planting superhero.

Now I know that it seems a little late for introductions, but it's time to officially meet the apostle Paul.

For starters, his name was actually Saul, Saul of Tarsus to be more specific. Saul was also a Jew but not your average Jew. Saul was one of the highest-ranking religious guys of his day. He belonged to a group called the Pharisees who strictly upheld the rules and laws of Judaism.

Saul also hated Christians. As a Jew, Saul believed that Jesus was an imposter, a false prophet who was leading the Jews away from the only God and into a false faith. Saul hated Christians so much that he not only had them arrested, he also had them executed.

The first time we see Saul in scripture, he was overseeing the stoning of a man named Stephen. Yes, Saul's followers literally threw rocks at this man until he died.

We pick up Saul's story in the book of Acts chapter 9 immediately following the stoning of Stephen as Paul enters the **encounter** phase of the Peter Parker Process.

> *Meanwhile, Saul was still breathing out murderous threats against the Lord's disciples. He went to the high priest and asked him for letters to the synagogues in Damascus, so that if he found any there who belonged to the Way, whether men or women, he might take them as prisoners to Jerusalem. As he neared Damascus on his journey, suddenly a light from heaven flashed around him. He fell to the*

ground and heard a voice say to him, "Saul, Saul, why do you persecute me?"

"Who are you, Lord?" Saul asked.

"I am Jesus, whom you are persecuting," he replied. "Now get up and go into the city, and you will be told what you must do."

The men traveling with Saul stood there speechless; they heard the sound but did not see anyone. Saul got up from the ground, but when he opened his eyes he could see nothing. So they led him by the hand into Damascus. For three days he was blind, and did not eat or drink anything. (Acts 9:1–6)

Can you imagine arresting and murdering people because they believed that Jesus was the Messiah and then meeting the man yourself? What do you say in that moment?

"I'm sorry for killing your followers" doesn't seem to cut it, but Saul doesn't even say that. Instead, he asks a question that leads to the identity of the very person Saul had been persecuting.

I would have been terrified!

However, God's grace and mercy are on full display through this powerful encounter. Instead of killing Saul, the resurrected Savior spares his life and reveals that he is in fact the Christ. Saul had no other choice but to believe in Jesus.

What a change of events!

Suddenly, in a split second, Saul knew that he was definitively wrong about his beliefs and needed to repent or "change his mind."

This was an impact moment that would forever change the life of Saul.

Just as Peter Parker's life was transformed after an encounter with a radioactive spider bite, Saul's transformation started by encountering Jesus Christ.

But Saul's encounter was just the beginning. Remember, the next phase of the Peter Parker Process is **empower**.

After Saul is blinded through his encounter with Jesus, he is told to enter the city of Damascus. And as Saul approaches Damascus, God sends a man named Ananias to pray for him. Check out what happens next in Acts 9:10–17:

> *Then Ananias went to the house and entered it. Placing his hands on Saul, he said, "Brother Saul, the Lord—Jesus, who appeared to you on the road as you were coming here—has sent me so that you may see again and be filled with the Holy Spirit." Immediately, something like scales fell from Saul's eyes, and he could see again. He got up and was baptized, and after taking some food, he regained his strength.*

So Saul is blinded and brought to a house in Damascus. While waiting and fasting in that house, God brings a man named Ananias to not only pray for Saul's healing, but also to empower him with the Holy Spirit.

Ananias then prays for Saul, scales fall from his eyes, and Saul can now see and is also filled with the Holy Spirit.

If you're wondering what just happened, Saul received his inheritance.

How do we know?

Before Saul's encounter with the Holy Spirit, the only power Saul had was given to him by the high priest to arrest and imprison Christians. After his encounter, Saul, like Peter Parker, began to transform into a superhero. But not just any superhero, Saul began to look and act like Jesus.

Like Peter Parker, Saul's encounter changed everything about him, including his name. Saul the Pharisee became Paul the Apostle, which is how I will address him moving forward.

Besides a name change, what other evidence existed that Paul was different?

Like Jesus, Paul could now heal sick people. Not even Spider-Man could do that!

In scripture we see Paul healing people through prayer, yes; but even more miraculous, Paul could touch a piece of cloth and if a sick person touched the clothing that touched Paul, they would get completely healed (Acts 19:12).

Paul could also work miracles. There was a man who had been crippled from birth, had never walked a day in his life, and Paul publicly commanded the man to stand and he stood. Not only that, he began to walk. The crowd was so amazed that they thought Paul was the Greek god Hermes (Acts 14:8–19).

Another way that Paul was empowered was through the ability to disarm his enemies. In Acts 13:1–12, there was a sorcerer named Bar-Jesus who was trying to stop Paul from sharing the message of Jesus. How did Paul handle the situation? He blinded the man. Not with pepper spray, but with the power of the Holy Spirit. In the same way that Jesus blinded Saul, Paul now had the superpower to blind bad guys.

Paul could even command demons to come out of possessed people, just like Jesus.

Most impressively of all, Paul had the explosive power to preach. That's a joke; you'll get it in a second.

One night while preaching, Paul's sermon went so long that a young man named Eutychus fell asleep while sitting in a windowsill. The details here only foreshadow one thing.

Yep, Eutychus fell out the window. Three stories down!

Talk about a service stopper.

So Paul pauses his midnight preaching marathon and runs downstairs where the man's lifeless body is now lying.

Scripture says that Paul threw himself on the young man, wrapping his arms around him. Not sure where he learned that technique, but it worked. Then Paul says, "He's alive! Don't be alarmed."

I love this guy, so casual after such an incredible miracle. "Nothing to see here, people, just another resurrected once-dead guy."

Picking Eutychus off the ground, they went back upstairs and had dinner together. I wonder how many people had an appetite after that.

Anyway, in case you missed it, Paul now had the power to raise dead people. Watch out, Bruce Willis.

From healing power to resurrection power, it's sufficient to say that Paul now had more power than Spider-Man could ever dream of through the Holy Spirit.

It's important to remember that Paul received his inheritance through a process.

Before Paul worked a single miracle, he first had an encounter with Jesus, was then empowered by the Holy Spirit, and what did Paul do next?

Let's check it out in Acts 9:19.

> *Now for several days he was with the disciples who were at Damascus, and immediately he began to proclaim Jesus in the synagogues, saying, "He is the Son of God." But Saul kept increasing in strength and confounding the Jews who lived at Damascus by proving that this Jesus is the Christ. (Acts 9:19–20, 22 NASB)*

The next phase in the Peter Parker Process is **exercise**.

Paul immediately exercised his inheritance by putting the power of God into practice.

When did he do that? From Acts 9:19–20, we don't read anything about Paul working a miracle.

Or do we?

The passage above from Acts 9:19 says that Paul immediately began to proclaim Jesus and prove that he is Christ, the Savior and Messiah.

If that doesn't make sense, let this sink in.

In his letter to the church in Rome, Paul says, "*I am unashamed of the gospel because it is the power of God that brings salvation to everyone who believes*" (Rom. 1:16).

Do you see it? Did you catch that?

Right there in the middle of Paul's message is the "power of God." The word *power*, again, is translated from the Greek *dunamis*.

And boom goes the dynamite!

The gospel—the message of Jesus and his perfect life, sacrificial and substitutionary death, and miraculous resurrection for the payment of sin—is the power of God that saves people.

What type of power?

Healing power, delivering power, resurrection power, dunamis power—all there in the gospel.

The gospel is power. Explosive power!

Miracles, signs, and wonders are great; but they are worthless without the gospel and the word of God. If Paul simply walked around healing the sick, raising the dead, and casting out demons but never shared the message of Jesus, it would be a total waste.

Why?

Because everyone is going to die some day of something. A miracle simply prolongs the inevitable. We are all going to die unless Jesus returns first.

But the gospel, the message of Jesus, contains the power of salvation.

Salvation from what?

Eternal separation from God, aka hell, a place of never-ending torment because of our sin.

Imagine the experience of Jesus on the cross lasting forever. An eternity of torture. That's what is at stake for the sinner. It's that serious.

Our sin was so serious that the Son of God, Jesus Christ, to set us free, to pay the penalty for sin, allowed himself to be arrested; beaten; stripped naked; humiliated; publicly lacerated; gashed with glass, stone; and bone ripping the flesh off his back before being nailed to a wooden crossbeam and lifted into the air, hanging there to be mocked and ridiculed until he released his Spirit through his final breath.

The cross is a reminder of what could have been.

It should have been us, beaten, hanging there, body bare; but God, in love, to fulfill all justice and to make us righteous, substituted himself.

Jesus died in our place for our sin and then rose from the dead defeating death, hell, and the grave. Jesus forever closed the gap between God and man, for those who believe.

Jesus took what we deserved to give us what we didn't. Eternal death traded for eternal life, aka "the great exchange," and greatest gift God has ever given.

That is good news.

"For God so loved the world, that he gave his one and only Son, that whoever believes in him will not perish, but will inherit everlasting life" (John 3:16).

And that is the power of God displayed through the gospel.

So Paul immediately put his inheritance into practice, and God's word says in Acts 9:22: *"That Saul kept increasing in strength."* That's what exercise does. The more you do it, the more you grow through it. Yes, Paul was already empowered through the Holy Spirit, but he was strengthened as he exercised his inheritance.

After encountering Jesus, being empowered by the Holy Spirit, and exercising his inheritance by sharing the message about the Messiah, Paul then entered the final phase of the Peter Parker Process and was **employed** by God. We read this in Acts 13:2–3: *"While they were ministering to the Lord and fasting, the Holy Spirit said, 'Set apart for Me Barnabas and Saul for the work to which I have called them.' Then, when they had fasted and prayed and laid their hands on them, they sent them away."*

Where was Paul sent? Wherever the Holy Spirit led him.

The **employ** stage of the Peter Parker Process is where Paul was set apart for the work of God.

What type of work specifically?

Soon after Jesus resurrected and right before he returned to heaven, Jesus gave his disciples their job description called the Great Commission. Jesus said, *"Go and make disciples of all nations, baptizing them in the name of the Father and of the Son and of the Holy Spirit, and teaching them to obey everything I have commanded you"* (Matt. 28:19–20).

We'll unpack this in a few pages, but Jesus is saying that we are basically employed by God to help people through the Peter Parker Process.

It's true!

God has given us an inheritance to help people encounter Jesus, become empowered by the Holy Spirit, exercise all that Jesus taught, and employ into a life of supernatural power as we repeat the process with others.

At this point, you're either amped about receiving your inheritance or still skeptical. For those who think that the Paul story seems as likely as Spider-Man swinging through their city, the next chapter is for you.

CHAPTER 4

Peter Parker Process
Phase 1: Encounter

For Peter Parker, it was a spider bite. In Bruce Wayne's experience, it was a bat. For another Bruce, the Hulk, aka Bruce Banner, it was a radioactive bomb blast. To Jesus, it was a supernatural bird.

There are various ways that superheroes receive their power, but many of them occurred through an encounter.

As I mentioned earlier and also in my previous book *From Mushrooms to the Messiah*, I received my inheritance in college through an encounter with Jesus Christ.

After expressing his love, addressing my sin, and calling me to repent and follow him, God gave me the Holy Spirit.

It happened while sitting in an apartment high on hallucinogenic drugs. Yes, I know, great start to a believable story. "I was high, and then I met God," but it's true! That's what happened.

Once high, now stone-cold sober, I heard the voice of the Lord. He sounded like a lion. With a voice that boomed through the living room, I sat there listening reverently having no idea what I was about to receive.

Scanning the room, wondering if I would see a physical manifestation of God's presence, a water bottle caught my eye.

It was an ordinary bottle of water: green plastic, black cap, and the brand Nalgene across the body.

Then it spoke.

Not the bottle, the voice of God. He said, "Drink of me and you will never thirst again."

It was a familiar sentence, one that resonated in my spirit.

As I thought about those words, I realized that Jesus said the same thing to a Samaritan woman at a water well in John 4 from the Bible. Sharing a similar experience with that woman, I sat in awe as God acknowledged that he knew all of my sin. He knew that I was searching for something to quench my thirst, something that I couldn't find in the pleasures of this world. God knew that I tried everything from substances to sex to steroids to success and none of them satisfied. He knew I was a desert of a man, empty, in a spiritual drought, desperate for a drink; and that is what the Lord was offering.

Living water.

Jesus said, "Let anyone who is thirsty come to me and drink. Whoever believes in me, as Scripture has said, rivers of living water will flow from within them" (John 7:37–38).

This wasn't one-time well water. Through the Holy Spirit, Jesus was offering rivers of living water, a continual flow that would never run dry and completely satisfy.

I needed that water.

Taking the bottle into my hands, I unscrewed the cap. Heart pounding with anticipation, I allowed the contents to escape. Into my mouth the water flowed, but this was not simply H_2O. I could feel something covering my body like a flood, quenching not just my physical thirst, but the deepest spiritual longings of my suffering soul.

The Holy Spirit did not descend on me like a dove; he came like a current that washed over me like living, electrifying water. I felt the power of God surging through my body, bringing what was once dead back to life. After that sip, I was revived, resurrected, and resuscitated.

Although I didn't have words to label what had just happened, Jesus filled me with the Holy Spirit. I was spiritually full. For the first time in my life, I was satisfied, both physically and spiritually. There was also the feeling of renewal, that I was different, changed, and transformed.

God's word provides the perfect description: *"If anyone is in Christ, the new creation has come: The old has gone, the new is here!"* (2 Cor. 5:17). My old self was dead and gone, buried in the waters of spiritual baptism; reborn; forgiven; and free.

Thankfully, Jesus had words to describe this as well. When approached by a famous Pharisee named Nicodemus, Jesus informed him that *"no one can see the kingdom of God unless they are born again"* (John 3:3). Confused by the statement, Nicodemus asked for an explanation, to which Jesus replied, *"Very truly I tell you, no one can enter the kingdom of God unless they are born of water and the Spirit. Flesh gives birth to flesh, but the Spirit gives birth to spirit"* (John 3:5–6).

To receive my inheritance, I had to be born again. I needed a new birth, a birth of water and spirit.

Like Saul, through my encounter with Jesus and the Holy Spirit, I was given that spiritual rebirth, along with a new nature, a super-nature. How did I know?

For starters, every addiction ended immediately. Where I was once enslaved to pornography, sex, substances, and insecurity, God instantly set me free. I didn't attend a single counseling session, addiction support group, or rehabilitation program. Instead, Jesus enrolled me in his one-step delivery plan where he gave me a new heart, new mind, new nature, new everything including the presence of his Spirit. The same Spirit that inhabited Jesus while He walked the earth two thousand years ago was now my inheritance.

I also knew I was different because the harmful things I once hungered for lost their allure. Instead of desiring to party and pursue women, I started to pray and pursue God's word. I couldn't put the book down. I developed an insatiable appetite to know God, and I honestly couldn't get enough. During my senior spring semester in college, I read the Bible cover to cover in three short months. I was obsessed with the word of God.

It's one thing to theoretically know that God exists, but to know him experientially by spending time in his presence is another level of pleasure altogether. Nothing compares. You will have to "taste and see" for yourself to know what I'm talking about.

My inheritance was also evident through my inability to stop talking about Jesus. Everyone needed to know what I now knew. I couldn't shut up about Jesus, my Savior. What some would say was obnoxious, the Bible called boldness. It didn't matter if I was at a bar or the gym bathroom, people were going to hear the good news.

After my encounter, I also discovered that I was empowered.

Paintball Party

It was a normal Saturday afternoon. There were no radioactive spider bites, toxic-waste spills, lightning strikes, freak accidents, nothing out of the ordinary. I was simply playing paintball with my fraternity brothers when it happened.

With eyes full of tears and red face from crying, my brother Mike approached me with some disturbing news.

"The doctors said I have six to twelve months left."

Having no context for his comment, I asked for clarification. "What do you mean six to twelve months left?"

With his head hanging downward staring at the ground, Mike was barely able to choke out his answer. "I'm dying. The doctors gave me six to twelve months to live."

Mike had a terminal heart condition. Until this moment I had no idea anything was wrong with him. However, Mike's meds were no longer a match for the death sentence dealt by his doctors.

What do you say in a moment like that? I didn't know.

That's when I heard it.

The same voice that called me to leave my life of sin behind to follow Jesus spoke again. For the second time in my life, I heard the voice of God.

"Matt, pray for Mike."

Knowing that Mike didn't believe in God made this a difficult task. "Are you sure, God?" I asked.

"Yes, I'm sure. Pray for him."

I asked Mike to talk with me privately. He followed me to a nearby bench where Mike continued to cry. After calming him down, I asked him the boldest question I've ever asked at that point in my life.

"Mike, can I pray for you?"

Mike looked at me with hopelessness in his eyes, but he affirmed my request.

Having no idea what to do or say, I took a step into the unknown and God met me there.

"Place your hand on his heart and ask me out loud to heal him," he said.

I first asked Mike for permission. He accepted, so I placed my hand on his heart.

It was a simple prayer: "God, thank you for Mike. I ask that you heal his heart and let him know that you are real and that you love him."

That was it.

There was no magic wand waiving, chanting, fairy dust sprinkling, or anything else you may have seen in the movies.

Honest speaking, I didn't know if anything had happened. Mike looked the same, sounded the same, reportedly felt the same, and I did too. However, something did happen that day. As I write this book, more than ten years later, Mike is still alive.

One simple prayer, prompted by God, empowered by the Spirit, brought a man from the brink of death into new life.

This was my explosive inheritance in action.

No amount of money, sex, drugs, or anything else could compare to the joy I felt from participating in that healing miracle. However, that wouldn't have happened without my baptism in the Holy Spirit. Like Peter Parker before the spider bite, I was just a man, but after my baptism in the Holy Spirit, I inherited the supernatural power of God.

To receive your inheritance, the first step in the Peter Parker Process is to encounter the saving power of Jesus Christ. Without coming to the realization that you are a sinner in need of a savior, without receiving forgiveness from God by placing your trust in the finished work of Jesus on the cross, the chances of you receiving an inheritance other than an eternity in hell are as good as seeing Spider-Man sitting in your living room watching the nightly news.

Sorry for being so blunt, but it's true.

Without Jesus, you are not only powerless, you're also headed for hell, an eternity of torment, separated from the God who loves you and gave his Son to save you. However...

God promises that if you call on the name of Jesus, confessing with your mouth that Jesus is Lord and believing in your heart that God raised him from the dead, you will be saved (Rom. 10:9). That's a guarantee!

In fact, God so badly wants to save you that he repeats the offer over and over again throughout the Bible: "If you confess your sins, God is faithful and just to forgive your sins and cleanse you from all unrighteousness" (1 John 1:9). I can go on and on with quotes about God's desire to forgive you, but the request has to come from you.

So if you have never asked Jesus to save you from sin, selfishness, Satan, and separation from God, today is your day. Right now, this opportunity is for you.

Some people want a scripted salvation prayer, but God doesn't give us one in his Word. Why?

When drowning, it doesn't matter how your cry for help sounds. If you call, your lifeguard will swim out to save you. It's the same with Jesus. Just call out! Cry if you have to. God is listening. Call out to Jesus, ask him to become your Lord and Savior, and he will come.

But wait, there's more!

Your encounter with Jesus will not only come with salvation, God will also give you his Holy Spirit. Paul tells us, *"When you believed, you were marked in him with a seal, the promised Holy Spirit, who is a deposit guaranteeing our inheritance..." (Eph. 1:13–14).*

There's that *inheritance* word again. Your encounter with Jesus comes with the inheritance of the Holy Spirit!

So you have encountered Jesus and received the Holy Spirit, now what? And when do the webs come?

Before you start seeking out the nearest skyscraper, follow me into the empower phase of the Peter Parker Process.

CHAPTER 5

Peter Parker Process
Phase 2: Empower

As we move along the Peter Parker Process, here's a quick recap of where we have been so far with our brother Saul.

On the road to Damascus, Saul had an encounter with Jesus. He heard his voice and was then blinded by the light that came from heaven. In Saul's encounter with Jesus, he was also told to wait in Damascus for further instructions. As we recently read, those instructions came from Ananias, who explained to Saul that God wanted to fill him with the Holy Spirit.

So Saul encountered Jesus but was not empowered and did not receive his inheritance until he was filled with the Holy Spirit. The moment Saul received his inheritance, his blinded eyes were opened and he was strengthened. Saul's life was then totally transformed. From that point forward, Saul would use his Greek name Paul as he experienced God's gifts, shared the gospel, and lived an empowered life like Jesus.

I realize that many books have been written about spiritual gifts, which is why I have been so hesitant to touch the subject, but I believe I'm bringing a unique life experience and biblical perspective to help you understand what God wants to give you.

I was not raised in a charismatic, Pentecostal, or "Spirit-filled" church. In fact, I never heard about the Holy Spirit while growing up in my family's church, let alone the gifts or baptism of the Holy Spirit.

Even after encountering Jesus and having such a powerful experience with the Holy Spirit, I did not have the vocabulary to describe that I had been baptized in the Holy Spirit. That language and those words were completely foreign to me.

All I knew was that, like Saul, I heard the voice of God, was filled with the Holy Spirit, and my life started to look like Jesus, including the miracles that I was reading about in God's word.

Then about nine months later, God brought me a mentor. He was an amazing man who partnered with God to help me heal from my past life before knowing Christ and become the man I needed to be for ministry.

In our mentorship, this man took me around the world on various trips where I discovered many new cultures and things about God's kingdom.

One thing I'll never forget about my mentor is that he would always find a Chinese food restaurant no matter which part of the world we were visiting.

In fact, we were sitting in a Chinese food restaurant in Switzerland of all places, when I first heard about the Baptism in the Holy Spirit.

My mentor said that God wanted to give me power that could only come once I had received this "specific" baptism.

I say "specific baptism" because he was not talking about being immersed in water. That already happened for me in high school. Instead, my mentor told me about the inheritance that God wanted to gift me through a spiritual baptism.

I did not understand what he meant by spiritual baptism, but as he described the benefits, I could feel an excitement bubbling up in my bones. I thought, *If I had these gifts and this power, I would literally be a real-life superhero!*

I started dreaming about having the power of Jesus to heal the sick, raise the dead, cast out demons, and perform the physics-defying miracles that I read about in the Bible. Our conversation actually brought me back to the blue binder of comic cards from my childhood. The world of supernatural abilities that I once regarded as fantasy was now becoming a reality.

My mentor asked if I wanted this gift from God.

Is the pope Catholic? I laughed to myself. I've never wanted something so badly in my life.

I'm sure he couldn't tell because I was trying to appear calm and collected, but every cell in my body wanted to yell, "Yes! I want it!"

He told me that we would pray after dinner and that I would know that I had received the gift when I spoke in tongues.

So we went back to the hotel and prayed.

And prayed.

And prayed and prayed.

For four hours we prayed.

Four hours!

Over and over we asked the Holy Spirit to baptize me, fill me, overflow in my life, and give me the gifts God had promised.

We even read the account of Pentecost from the book of Acts chapter 2 when Jesus first baptized his apostles with the Holy Spirit. I was half expecting that tongues of fire would fall from the hotel ceiling like they did on the day of Pentecost, but they didn't.

Nothing seemed to have happened that night.

Well, that's not entirely true, while we were praying, a volcano erupted in Iceland that disrupted all flights around Europe, including ours, but I didn't speak in tongues and therefore wasn't baptized in the Holy Spirit.

I was disappointed but also determined.

Jesus promised, "Your Father in heaven will give the Holy Spirit to those who ask him" (Luke 11:13).

I was asking.

For four hours I was asking!

Since God's promises are perfect, I thought it was possible that I wasn't asking in the right way.

I became driven to discover the key to unlocking this great mystery, and I wouldn't stop until I spoke in tongues.

If only I had gone to God's word to study this subject myself instead of chasing an experience, I would have saved so much time and heartache. Instead, I experienced a spiritually destructive season where I became religious and neglected my relationship with God. Instead of pursuing the Giver, I pursued the gift. I was focused on a specific result instead of our relationship.

During that time, I visited a variety of churches who regularly spoke about the Holy Spirit. From these churches I had countless people pray for me to receive the baptism in the Spirit and all the accompanying gifts from God. I was also doing my part by personally asking, praying, and pleading with God—to no avail.

Why wasn't this happening?

Was something wrong with me?

Did I not have enough faith?

Was there a sin issue in my life?

I know that God is a good Father, was I not mature enough to handle the Holy Spirit?

What was going on?

These unanswered questions turned my disappointment into discouragement, which eventually evolved into a spiritual depression.

Looking back, I now realize that I had adopted a merit-based mindset. I thought if God hasn't baptized me and given me these gifts, it's because I haven't earned it yet. So I started seeking God's gifts through religious works. I thought if I served enough, prayed enough, fasted enough, gave enough, God would baptize and bless me.

Gifts don't work like that and neither does God.

If you work to receive something, that's not a gift, it's a reward. The Bible never describes the "rewards of the spirit" only "gifts of the spirit."

Gifts are given and received, not earned or awarded.

We give gifts in love, not obligation.

If I work for someone, they are obligated to pay me.

In relationship, I am not obligated to give gifts. I do that in love.

Despite the logic, I continued my religious pursuit of the elusive gift of tongues. I remember attending a couple churches that put speaking in tongues on such a pedestal that they claimed it was proof of salvation. Yes, I heard it taught that the gift of tongues was not only a proof of your baptism in the Holy Spirit but evidence that you were saved!

That was new. I had never heard that one before.

I knew it wasn't true, but it made me question.

The questions also came with feeling like a second-class Christian, that something was missing, that I was incomplete. I began to believe something was sincerely wrong with me, that I wasn't pleasing to God enough for him to give me this gift.

Although I never walked away from Jesus, I eventually stopped seeking the baptism. If God didn't want me to have it, fine.

Eventually, the questioning grew quiet and I stopped caring, stopped pursuing.

I was tired of thinking that I wasn't enough, so I stopped thinking about it altogether.

Life went on.

The More of God...

A few years later I married my best friend. She was beautiful, godly, perfect for me in every way; but we couldn't agree on one thing.

From the time we started dating until we finally got married four years later, I was attending a church that she did not like.

We would walk away from a Sunday morning service, and she would say, "Church was okay, but something is missing."

When pressing her to define that "something," she couldn't put it into words. Instead, she vaguely explained that there was just "more."

"More?" I would ask. "What do you mean by more?"

When she wouldn't explain, I started to make assumptions. "She won't explain it to me because she is a spiritual snob and thinks I'm a second-class Christian who can't speak in tongues like she does!"

Now, my wife would have never said or thought those things, but the religious rat race that I willingly entered into was messing with my mind.

You see, my wife received the gift of tongues while being baptized in the Holy Spirit. She never boasted about it and was instead supportive and encouraging about me seeking the same. My wife even made a practice of encouraging me to pursue God's presence instead of his presents.

As we pursued God together in this way, we came to the conclusion that we needed to find a church that wouldn't simply teach about God, but also would encourage us to experience him through the Holy Spirit.

After a few months of searching, God brought us to our new church home. It was there where I regularly heard teachings on the Holy Spirit, God's gifts, and, of course, the spiritual baptism. The hunger in my heart began to grow again for the inheritance. However, this time would be different. Instead of seeking an experience, I sought God's word. I did what I should have done four years before and went to the Bible to see what it actually said on the subject.

What I discovered astounded me.

Everything that I read in the Bible pointed me back to the fact that I had already been baptized in the Holy Spirit!

Specifically in 1 Corinthians 12:13, I read, "For in one Spirit we were all baptized into one body—Jews or Greeks, slaves or free—and all were made to drink of one Spirit."

We were all made to drink of the one Spirit!

It finally clicked.

The night of the Nalgene water bottle, the night in college when I heard the voice of the Lord, the night when a current of electrifying power surged through my system, the Holy Spirit baptized me!

I drank of the Holy Spirit!

He inhabited me.

I had already inherited him!

I was baptized in the Holy Spirit and sealed by him for salvation the moment I believed (Eph. 1:13–14; 1 Cor. 12:13; Eph. 4:4–5).

How did I know?

What evidence was there?

Could I speak in tongues? No.

Was my life radically transformed like Saul? Yes!

Did I now have the boldness to share Jesus? Yes!

Was God speaking to me prophetically and healing people through me? Yes!

The Bible actually teaches about "fruit of the spirit" or evidences that our tree is producing what God wants to see. From Galatians 5:22, the fruit of the spirit is love, joy, peace, patience, kindness, goodness, faithfulness, gentleness, and self-control (Gal. 5:22). After my baptism in the Holy Spirit, those fruits were there but I was so blinded by what I didn't have that I couldn't see the fruit through the trees.

I now realized what Adam and Eve must have felt like.

They had access to everything in the Garden of Eden, but the lie from the snake said, because they didn't have one fruit, God wasn't good and was withholding from them.

How blinded they must have been.

By focusing on what they couldn't have, they lost sight of all that belonged to them.

Blinded by unbelief, Adam and Eve listened to that lie, rebelled against God, pursued the forbidden fruit, broke God's command, and shattered their relationship with him.

I was on the same path.

God had given me his Holy Spirit; sealed me for salvation; and empowered me to heal, prophesy, work miracles, and hear his voice from heaven. But I bought into the lie that tongues, the one fruit I didn't have, was worth forsaking all the other fruits I did have.

For years, while pursuing the gift of tongues, I completely neglected the other gifts. Like Saul, I was blind! I was blind to the goodness of God, blind to his generosity, and blind to his grace. I was also blind to the fact that God had already gifted me with an inheritance in the Holy Spirit.

But my eyes were opened. The truth of God's word filled my mind until I could clearly see that I had been deceived.

So you know what I did?

I repented.

Then I got water baptized.

Why?

I wanted to remember the day that I received the Holy Spirit's baptism. I wanted to commemorate the day I decided to follow Jesus. I desired to submit to the instruction of Christ to publicly identify with his death, burial, and resurrection. I wanted to declare that I was different, and the old Matt was truly dead and gone.

So I was baptized in water and baptized in the spirit, but I still didn't speak in tongues. Yet for the first time, I didn't care. I was content knowing the truth.

What truth?

The Bible teaches that the Holy Spirit determines which gifts each person will receive:

> *To one there is given through the Spirit a message of wisdom, to another a message of knowledge by means of the same Spirit, to another faith by the same Spirit, to another gifts of healing by that one Spirit, to another miraculous powers, to another prophecy, to another distinguishing between spirits, to another speaking in different kinds of tongues, and to still another the interpretation of tongues. All these are the work of one and the same Spirit, and he distributes them to each one, just as he determines. (1 Cor. 12:8–11)*

Several verses later in the same chapter, Paul asks a rhetorical question to solidify that the Holy Spirit does not give all the same gifts to all the same people: *"Are all apostles? Are all prophets? Are all teachers? Do all work miracles? Do all have gifts of healing? Do all speak in tongues? Do all interpret"* (1 Cor. 12:29–30).

The answer to Paul's question is, of course, no. Not everyone receives the same gifts.

However, if it were up to Paul, we would all speak in tongues but we don't. Instead, Paul prefers that we prophesy (1 Cor. 14:5). Again, this is not up to Paul, it's the Holy Spirit who distributes his gifts as he determines.

God's word teaches that we do not all have the same gifts, but we are all part of the same body and every part is important (1 Cor. 12:12–31). Every part of the church is called and equipped for ministry, but they may operate in different gifts to fulfill their function.

Does that mean any are of less value?

Of course not!

You are not less than because you lack a specific gift. If God wants you to have it, you will. He has his reasons and his timing. Learn to trust that "His ways are higher than our ways and his thoughts are higher than our thoughts" (Isa. 55:8–9). Furthermore, "Our God is in the heavens, he does whatever he pleases" (Ps. 115:3). God is a good Father and a generous giver. He loves his kids and gives good gifts.

Bottom-line, if you want a gift, ask. Pursue the Gift Giver. Jesus said, *"If you then, though you are evil, know how to give good gifts to your children, how much more will your Father in heaven give the Holy Spirit to those who ask him!"* (Luke 11:13).

The power comes from the Holy Spirit, and the Holy Spirit determines which gifts we get, but we are still encouraged to desire the ones we want: "Follow the way of love and eagerly desire the gifts of the Spirit, especially prophecy" (1 Cor. 14:1). This is Paul telling us to not simply desire the gifts of the Spirit, but to get specific.

However, "hurry up and wait" is the name of the asking game. I actually wouldn't end up receiving the gift of tongues for another three years after my water baptism, seven years after asking for the gift and ten years after being baptized in the Holy Spirit.

It happened on my thirty-second birthday when my wife and two friends took me to the Grand Canyon. After gazing at the beauty of God's creation, we sat in a circle overlooking the gorge and prayed for God to gift me with tongues.

It was a familiar scene: they prayed, asked, spoke in tongues, prophesied, but nothing seemed to happen to me.

Then I walked away from the prayer circle, took another look at the beautiful canyon, and it hit me.

A still, small voice with one single syllable.

I began to repeat it over and over again in my head until the words came out of my mouth. Not sure if this was tongues, I kept quiet and continued to practice under my breath. Walking from the Grand Canyon to the car and all the way back to our hotel, I was praying to God in an unknown language.

Finally!

All of that waiting, totally worth it.

It's true when the Bible says that, "Every good and perfect gift is from above, coming down from the Father of the heavenly lights" (James 1:17). I was overwhelmed with the goodness and grace of God, receiving this gift with my wife and best friends at the Grand Canyon of all places. It made perfect sense. God's divine timing is perfect every time.

Now, the purpose of sharing this history was to point out that our explosive inheritance, the power of God comes through the baptism with the Holy Spirit. What that looks like and how it happens differs from experience to experience, but the same type of fruits follows: freedom from sin; boldness to share the gospel; manifestations of God's power, miracles, signs, wonders, prophecy, tongues, etc.

Interestingly enough, there is a lot of disagreement and controversy surrounding the baptism with the Holy Spirit. Mainly because people are not actually reading what the Bible says contextually. So let's take a closer look at the biblical means through which our dunamis power is delivered.

The Holy Spirit's Baptism: A Brief History

In the New Testament, John the Baptist was the first person to mention the baptism with the Holy Spirit. John got his name because he spent his life baptizing people for the repentance of their sin and preparation to receive the lordship of the coming Messiah. Then, right before Jesus comes to John to be baptized, John said, *"I baptize you with water for repentance. But after me comes one who is more powerful than I, whose sandals I am not worthy to carry. He will baptize you with the Holy Spirit and fire"* (Matt. 3:11).

There it is—"Jesus will baptize you with the Holy Spirit and fire." That's what John the Baptist said.

Jesus then gets baptized by John and receives the Holy Spirit, who descends on him in the form of a dove. At the same time as Jesus is praying, heaven opens and the voice of the Father said, "You are my Son, whom I love; with you I am well pleased" (Luke 3:21–22). Then the Bible says, "Jesus, full of the Holy Spirit, left the Jordan (where he was baptized) and was led by the Spirit into the wilderness."

Quick recap. Jesus is baptized, receives the Holy Spirit, and is now "full" of the Holy Spirit.

He then goes into the desert for forty days and nights to fast, pray, and resist the temptation of Satan. When Jesus leaves the desert to start his public ministry, the Bible says that *Jesus returned to Galilee in the power of the Spirit*" (Luke 4:14).

Again, Jesus was baptized, received the Holy Spirit, is full of the Holy Spirit; and then after his time in the desert, Jesus is described as having the power of the Spirit.

We then read throughout the gospel accounts in Matthew, Mark, Luke, and John that Jesus began to teach a message of repentance while demonstrating that he is the Messiah and Savior of the world through countless miracles, signs, and wonders. So many that John said, *"If every one of them were written down, I suppose that even the whole world would not have enough room for the books that would be written"* (John 21:25).

Jesus is then crucified, dies, and, three days later, rises from the dead just as he said.

The day that Jesus resurrected, on Easter Sunday, he went to visit his disciples. Jesus found them behind locked doors, hiding for fear of the Jewish leaders. Jesus did not have a key, he did not knock, and the door was not opened for him. Instead, Jesus appeared in the room. Did he walk through the wall? We don't know. What we do know is this, Jesus shows the disciples his hands and feet that were recently nailed to a wooden cross, commissions them, and then he does something peculiar.

The Bible says that Jesus breathed on them and said, "Receive the Holy Spirit" (John 20:22).

As I read this account, I'm thinking what that must have looked like for Jesus to breathe on them? Also, why was that an important detail?

Did he blow on them back and forth like an oscillating fan? Did he exhale the Spirit like he did when he gave up his life on the cross?

Again, we don't know.

However, whatever Jesus did by breathing on the disciples was important enough to record in the canon of scripture.

Context is key.

In John chapter 3, Jesus is having a conversation with a Pharisee named Nicodemus. In that conversation Jesus tells Nicodemus that people must be born again to enter the kingdom of God.

Key point: to enter the kingdom of God, we must be born again.

What happened when the first person, Adam, was born?

Wait.

He wasn't born, not in the traditional sense.

In Genesis 2:7, the Bible says, "Then the LORD God formed a man from the dust of the ground and breathed into his nostrils the breath of life, and the man became a living being."

Did you catch that?

God brought about the first birth, the first person, the first creation by breathing life into him.

This starts to make sense when considering Jesus's conversation with Nicodemus. "You must be born again." Paul says it this way: "If anyone is in Christ, he is a new creation" (2 Cor. 5:17).

Watch this!

God brings the first man to life through his breath, and Jesus breathes on his disciples so that they are born again. Not only that, the disciples received the Holy Spirit at the same time!

Paul's writing to the church in Ephesus now makes sense: *"You also were included in Christ when you heard the message of truth, the gospel of your salvation. When you believed, you were marked in him with a seal, the promised Holy Spirit, who is a deposit guaranteeing our inheritance until the redemption of those who are God's possession—to the praise of his glory" (Eph. 1:13–14).*

The disciples were born again and sealed with the Spirit at the same time.

Are you tracking with me?

This is so important. Don't miss this!

In John 20, Jesus breathes on his disciples. They are born again and receive the Holy Spirit. Then Jesus says this: "I am going to send you what my Father has promised; but stay in the city until you have been clothed with power from on high" (Luke 24:49).

Jesus is also recorded having the same conversation in Acts 1:4–5: *"Do not leave Jerusalem, but wait for the gift my Father promised, which you have heard me speak about. For John baptized with water, but in a few days you will be baptized with the Holy Spirit."*

The disciples already received the Holy Spirit when Jesus breathed on them, but in the same breath, Jesus says that they still needed power.

How would they receive this power?

Jesus said that they needed to be baptized with the Holy Spirit.

I find it odd that the disciples could have the Holy Spirit and still lack power. There must be something to this baptism with the Holy Spirit that is different than simply receiving the Holy Spirit upon salvation and rebirth.

Which brings us to the Day of Pentecost in Acts chapter 2:

> *When the day of Pentecost came, they were all together in one place. Suddenly a sound like the blowing of a violent wind came from heaven and filled the whole house where they were sitting. They saw what seemed to be tongues of fire that separated and came to rest on each of them. All of them were filled with the Holy Spirit and began to speak in other tongues as the Spirit enabled them.* (Acts 2:1–4)

In John 20, the disciples received the Holy Spirit, and in Acts 2, they were baptized with the Holy Spirit.

Notice something though. Acts 2 does not say that the disciples were baptized. Instead, it says they were "filled" with the Holy Spirit.

Again, what Jesus described as a baptism, the writer and disciple Luke described as being filled.

Why the distinction? What's the difference?

Nothing!

The words are synonymous.

Being baptized with the Holy Spirit and being filled with the Holy Spirit are the same thing. Not only that, it happens multiple times to the same group of people!

What am I saying?

It wasn't a one-time experience!

On the Day of Pentecost in Acts 2, John and Peter were waiting in Jerusalem with the other disciples when they were all baptized or filled with the Holy Spirit.

Then, in Acts 4, Peter is again described as being full of the Spirit as he shares the gospel with a group of angry religious people.

Peter is then arrested along with John, and after their release, they return to their own people. As a group of believers, they all pray that God would equip and empower them to share the gospel boldly and perform the same miracles, signs, and wonders of Jesus.

This is an interesting prayer for people who were already described as being filled and baptized with the Holy Spirit. Why pray to be filled if you are already filled?

Isn't it obvious and redundant to continuously call them "filled with the Holy Spirit"?

It is unless it was a new filling each time.

Check this out.

When they were done praying, Acts 4:31 says, *"After they prayed, the place where they were meeting was shaken. And they were all filled with the Holy Spirit and spoke the word of God boldly."*

The Bible says that they were all filled with the Holy Spirit.

All includes Peter and John.

That is three times in four chapters that Peter is described as being filled with the Holy Spirit.

Why was he filled?

To answer that, let's take another look at Pentecost.

Fire Festival

Pentecost actually existed long before the baptism with the Holy Spirit happened. It was originally called the Festival of Weeks, a Jewish celebration of the harvest, which occurred on the seventh Sunday after Passover. When translated into Greek, this festival of weeks is called Pentecost.

God strategically planned the empowering of his people through the baptism with the Holy Spirit to occur on the Day of Pentecost as described in Acts chapter 2.

Why?

Let me quote Jesus to help connect the dots: *"The harvest is plentiful, but the laborers are few, therefore pray earnestly to the Lord of the harvest to send out laborers into his harvest"* (Matt. 9:38).

God was empowering his people for the harvest.

In fact, Jesus always intended his disciples to be harvesters of people just as he first called them to be fishers of men (Matt. 4:19). Whatever the job title, harvesters or fishermen, the purpose and product were always people. People are the harvest and the catch according to Jesus.

However, Jesus knew that his disciples needed power for the picking. They needed to be empowered by the Holy Spirit to harvest souls for the kingdom of God.

It's important to highlight that the Holy Spirit empowers us for ministry. Jesus said, *"You will receive power when the Holy Spirit comes on you; and you will be my witnesses in Jerusalem, and in all Judea and Samaria, and to the ends of the earth..."* (Acts 1:8). People were empowered to witness or testify to the truth. We'll talk more about this in the employ portion of the Peter Parker Process, but this principle will help us understand how ministry works.

When we, like Paul, see the power of God working in our lives, that is a fruit or evidence that we are filled with the Holy Spirit. The power does not come from us. The source is the Holy Spirit.

This is why the Bible tells us not to get drunk with wine but to be filled with the Holy Spirit (Eph. 5:18).

Just as it is possible to feel empowered by the effects of wine, the Holy Spirit empowers us to do things that would be otherwise impossible when spiritually sober.

I don't know about you, but I have a testimony! I wasn't always a pastor. At one time I thought that alcohol made me Superman, but now, it's only kryptonite when compared to the power of the Holy Spirit.

We are called to be filled with the Holy Spirit so that we can help others know the gospel through the power of God.

The Bible also tells us not to quench the Holy Spirit (1 Thess. 5:19).

When we quench a fire, it means that we have extinguished the flames. It is possible to extinguish the fire of the Holy Spirit in our lives. We can even offend or grieve the Holy Spirit (Eph. 4:30). Remember, he is a person. When we overtly sin or covertly ignore him, we can grieve him and consequently quench his flame.

To clarify, the Spirit of God never leaves us (Heb. 13:5), but we can leak.

In other words, over time, without constantly being refilled or baptized, we can see a diminished effect of the Spirit. It's true, without being full, our fire becomes dull.

This is why we are told be filled with the Holy Spirit. We constantly need the power of the Holy Spirit to fuel and fulfill our purpose. How can we be filled? Plug into the power source. All throughout Jesus's ministry, we see him working public miracles and then getting alone in private with his Father. If Jesus needed to recharge through relationship with his Father, then so do we.

Think of your spiritual life like a smartphone. The Holy Spirit has given you an inheritance of spiritual tools or apps, but they are powerless without plugging into the power source. What good is a smartphone with a dead battery? Besides weighing down paper, not much else. We too need to plug into the power source so we can effectively utilize the tools we have inherited.

Be filled by your Father. Spend time with him in the word of God and through worship, praise, prayer, silence, or any other spiritual practice that recharges your battery. Do this daily. God created us to need daily bread, and like the Israelites in the desert, God has fresh bread for us every day but we need to feed to stay full.

Every time I prepare to lay my hands on the sick, take the pulpit to preach, or share the gospel with someone at work, I pray to be filled with the power of the Spirit. When I am full, the Spirit is manifested, not Matt.

If there was a miracle, it wasn't Matt. I can promise you that.

Lastly, unlike a smartphone battery, we can be filled beyond 100 percent. That's when miracles, signs, and wonders work the best, through the overflow of power from our lives. God has power for us, but when we overflow, that power impacts others. And guess what? You can have as much of God as you want!

Some people are content connecting with God once a week at church. Others want to plug in multiple times per week through various Bible studies and life groups. Many more understand their daily need for God and connect with him Monday through Sunday, but the truth is, you can have as much of God as you want. There is an all-day, every-day, 24/7 buffet for those who want to feast in fellowship with God. The only person limiting your power level is you. It's time to plug in, power up, and watch the Holy Spirit work!

Unboxing God

As we recently discussed, your inheritance is received upon salvation through your encounter with Jesus. Again, you are sealed by the Holy Spirit the second that you are saved. However, the empowerment comes through your baptism or filling with the Holy Spirit.

Interestingly enough, as we read the account of the early church through the book of Acts, we see some people being baptized with the Holy Spirit at salvation and others at a separate time.

Why? The Bible does not allow us to put God in a box.

If God wants to save and empower you at the same time, that is his prerogative. However, if he has you wait for a season before baptizing you in the Spirit, that's also biblical. The disciples received the Holy Spirit in John 20 and were empowered at Pentecost ten days later.

In Acts 8, we read about a group of people from Samaria who believed in the gospel and were baptized with water in Jesus's name, but these people did not receive their inheritance at that time. It wasn't until Peter and John laid their hands on the Samaritans that they received the Holy Spirit.

Two chapters later, in Acts 10, Peter is preaching to a group of non-Jewish people called Gentiles, and as Peter spoke, the Holy Spirit filled the new believers. Simply by listening to the gospel and believing in the message, these people were baptized with Holy Spirit before their water baptism.

What was the evidence?

The Gentile believers were speaking in tongues, just as the disciples did at Pentecost. Then Peter said, *"Surely no one can stand in the way of their being baptized with water. They have received the Holy Spirit just as we have"* (Acts 10:47).

This was an important event in church history.

At Pentecost, only the Jewish followers of Jesus were baptized with the Holy Spirit, but Acts 10 demonstrates that any believer could be baptized with the Holy Spirit.

After all people had access to the Holy Spirit, the world would never be the same. Anyone who called on the name of Jesus, whether Jew or Gentile, could receive an inheritance from God.

That includes you and me!

If you're alive, you qualify.

Just as the Bible describes a variety of ways and times that people were baptized with the Holy Spirit, a simple survey of the church today will show you the same. Some people have been baptized with the Holy Spirit the second they believed. Others believed for many years before being baptized.

For example, my wife was saved and received the Holy Spirit as a young girl, but it wasn't until high school that she was filled.

How did she know?

She was instantaneously set free from her addiction to pornography and also began to speak in tongues. Her life was radically transformed after being empowered by the Holy Spirit.

Me, I was saved, sealed, and filled at the same time.

Today, both me and my wife work with the Holy Spirit to help people know our God and the gospel. It doesn't matter that our experiences were different; we have the same Holy Spirit.

God does not allow us to relegate his gifts to a set of religious rituals or requirements. If we could punch in a combination to receive the gifts, God would be a cosmic vending machine but he is not. God is a Father who gives good gifts to his kids, including an inheritance.

You have an inheritance! "Ask and you shall receive" (Matt. 7:7). That was Jesus, in case you were wondering. More specifically, Jesus said, "If you then, though you are evil, know how to give good gifts to your children, how much more will your Father in heaven give the Holy Spirit to those who ask him!" (Luke 11:13).

If you have not been baptized in the Holy Spirit, it's time to ask. Jesus encouraged us to ask on many occasions, including at least two parables that paint the picture of us persistently knocking until our prayers are answered (Luke 18:1–8, 11:5–13). Thankfully, receiving and being baptized with the Holy Spirit is a prayer that our Heavenly Father loves to answer. So ask!

Then, once you have encountered Jesus and been empowered by the Holy Spirit, like Peter Parker, it's time to put that power into practice.

Let's take some time in the next chapter to learn how to exercise our inheritance.

CHAPTER 6

Peter Parker Process
Phase 3: Exercise

A major part of my development in the dunamis power that God gifted me came through the exercise phase of the Peter Parker Process.

The exercise phase is where Peter Parker discovers his new power and equipment while learning how to use them. Again, this is where Peter Parker discovers that he can climb walls, crawl across ceilings, swing from trees, and shoot webs from his wrists. He wasn't perfect, but the more he practiced, Peter Parker became proficient and eventually professional, as Spider-Man.

When I first heard about my inheritance, that supernatural, dunamis power was available, I was obviously intrigued but I had no idea where to begin. So, like any person who wants to exercise, but doesn't know the difference between a dumbbell and a doorknob, I needed personal training. I needed someone to show me the ropes, someone to take me on a tour of the gym, walk me through the motions, ensure that I felt comfortable handling the new equipment and had proper form to fulfill my purpose without hurting any people in the process, including myself.

When I first started exercising, I watched how people used the equipment in the gym, I researched workouts online and in muscle magazines. I copied the routines of successful bodybuilders and asked for help from more experienced lifters.

There were many times that I needed someone to spot me on heavy lifts or show me how to perform new exercises, so I looked around for powerful people who were doing it well and asked for a hand. There was no need for me to reinvent the wheel, I just needed to find the people who had already achieved the goals I was seeking and simply replicate what they were doing.

Just as a personal trainer is highly recommended for any gym newcomer, a personal trainer or mentor is recommended to disciple you through the process of training to use your dunamis power.

Thankfully, my Heavenly Father already had a lengthy list of people who would train me to handle my inheritance:

My mentor was the first to teach me that the gifts existed. He opened my eyes to the fact that my Heavenly Father had superpowers available through the Holy Spirit that were my birthright as an adopted son of God.

My wife, Alissa, pushed me to pursue people who were proficient in the dunamis power of the Spirit. So I started listening to lessons and reading books on the dunamis power of God. I surrounded myself and learned from spiritually powerful people who knew how to handle their inheritance. I watched how they used their gifts and attempted to replicate their example. I again learned that there is no need to reinvent the wheel. Yes, God gave us creativity, but his Word set a standard. Jesus showed us the way and asked us to follow in his footsteps.

My church provided the training facility and many opportunities to put the power into practice. Specifically, my spiritual "gym" was the mission field and ministry at Sunday services and midweek Bible studies. Each place provided the support to succeed, the freedom to fail, and an environment to explore the dunamis power under the supervision of seasoned professionals.

Train to Test

I also learned how to discern the teachings that I was receiving. In the book of Acts, a group of people called the Bereans were applauded for their critical analysis. Acts 17:11 says, *"The Berean*

Jews were of more noble character than those in Thessalonica, for they received the message with great eagerness and examined the Scriptures every day to see if what Paul said was true."

Notice what the Bereans did here: they were eager to learn from people with more power and experience, like Paul, but they still compared any teaching to the word of God to determine if it was true.

It is good to eagerly desire the dunamis power of God. Paul tells us in 1 Corinthians 14:1, "Eagerly desire the gifts of the Spirit," but we need to test the teachings we receive. It is easy for people to twist scripture to fit personal agendas, misunderstand or errantly apply a text, teach something out of context, and ultimately mislead people to believe false teachings.

Too many people have fallen into the trap of false teaching because they follow powerful people without an understanding of what God's word says for themselves. We need to test the source material. As followers of Christ, it is okay and highly encouraged for us to be analytical and critical when it comes to teaching and preaching. God's word has set the standard by which we can test and prove whether a teaching is true or false.

Just because someone teaches about the power of God doesn't mean that they are godly. Just as someone who is godly may not teach on the dunamis power of God. I say this because there are many people who have taught me how to accurately and biblically apply the power of God whose teachings on other topics did not align with scripture. In those situations, my wife has taught me to "take the meat and leave the bones." In other words, "Don't throw the baby out with the bathwater."

If someone accurately teaches on the power of God, but misinterprets a different doctrine, does that mean that their teaching on the dunamis power was false? No. However, I know too many Christians who never read the word of God for themselves. Instead, they simply receive and believe anything taught from the pulpit with a blind, dogmatic trust that the pastor is teaching them biblical truth. We need to discern, based on the word of God, what to keep and what to discard.

How will you know unless you read the Bible yourself?

The truth is, there are people in my past who have inspired me to passionately pursue the power and presence of God whose teachings I won't follow today.

Their lives may have inspired me to pursue God, but their teachings didn't always line up with God's word.

Did that derail my pursuit of God or his dunamis power? No.

I sincerely thank those people for pointing me to God, but I now choose not to listen to their teachings.

The Ice-Cream Man

Imagine having never tried ice cream. Then you meet an extremely obese, unhealthy, seven-hundred-pound man eating an ice cream cone. The man hands you a cone, and you instantly enjoy the taste. Just because that man introduced you to something sweet and amazing does not mean that you are going to copy his lifestyle.

At some point that man took something good and started to abuse it.

It's okay to thank the man for showing you ice cream, but you don't need to follow in his footsteps.

Do you see what I'm saying here?

There are spiritually obese pastors, preachers, and teachers who will inspire you to "taste and see that the Lord is good" while teaching false doctrine. Yes, it's even possible for these spiritually powerful people to demonstrate dunamis power in their lives while twisting and abusing scripture. Does that mean you should disregard God? No.

The truth doesn't change because people misapply it. Truth is always true.

Instead, we need to learn to discern the truth and discard the false teaching (1 Thess. 5:21).

You can continue to enjoy the sweetness and goodness of God without falling for false teachings if you test all things with the truth of God's word.

Wolves in Wool

If you're like me, maybe you're asking, "How can people display dunamis power while teaching falsely and misleading people?"

There are a few things to consider. First...

Jesus warned us in Matthew 24:24 that false prophets will appear and perform great signs and wonders to deceive, if possible, even the elect. We were warned that this would happen, so we need to be on guard and test everything like the Bereans did.

Remember, not all power is God's power. Just because another religion has experiences with the supernatural does not mean that the power is coming from God. The devil and his demons also have power, and they use it deceptively. You can read about this in Exodus where almost every miracle of Moses was replicated by Pharaoh's magicians. God's word tells us, "Beloved, do not believe every spirit, but test the spirits to see whether they are from God, for many false prophets have gone out into the world" (1 John 4:1).

Second, God's word tells us that the gifts and the call are irrevocable (Rom. 11:29). God does not take away our gifts. It is possible for people to receive a gift and fall out of relationship with God, but that doesn't mean that God will take back the gift.

Third, we are told in 2 Corinthians 2:17 that many people will peddle the word of God for profit.

What does that mean?

People will take God's word, his gifts, and power using them to take money from people.

Jesus told his disciples, in reference to the gifts, "Freely you have received, now freely give."

Can you imagine the disciples setting up a stand at the entrance to the temple offering healings or prophecies for a price?

"Get your healing here! Just $5 per prayer! Healing here! Get your healing, just $5!"

Peddling healing prayers or prophecies like peanuts at the ballpark may sound ridiculous, but this is a modern-day reality. There are some really amazing evangelists on television, Internet, and at revivals across the world; but there are also those who want you to pay for your breakthrough, miracle, sign, or wonder. Watch out!

Biblically speaking, this never turns out well. Anytime we see people receiving or requesting payment for miracles, they are rebuked or cursed (see 2 Kings 5:15–27 or Acts 8:18–23).

Ultimately, Jesus tells us that we will know a tree by its fruit.

You will know a banana tree if it produces bananas.

What kind of fruit does the tree produce?

Test the tree for quality as well.

Just because a tree produces apples doesn't mean those are good apples. You can have a rotten apple tree.

In the same way, simply displaying dunamis power doesn't mean that someone's doctrine is good. Test the tree. Compare the fruit to the flawless word of God.

Please understand that I'm not encouraging a heretical witch hunt here. I'm simply saying that God's word needs to be your guide.

Learn to Discern

I've been asked to identify the false teachers that I've referenced in this book, and I'm sorry, but I refuse. My goal is to train you to have a critical and analytical mind, to think for yourselves, not to be blind sheep who listen to anyone's gospel except for God's.

Jesus said it best: "If you hold to my teaching, you are truly my disciples. You will know the truth and the truth will set your free" (John 8:31).

Ask anyone who has fallen for the lies of a cult if they feel free.

Jesus wants you to be protected from peddlers and false teachers so you can be free to enjoy him and the inheritance he has freely gifted you. Go to the source, test everything, and be free.

There are so many resources available today that can help us learn and discern what the Bible actually says, starting with the Bible. Most every Bible comes with a concordance. This resource is usually included in the back of the book and provides the location of specific words, themes, people, places, and things. My favorite form of concordance is found through the Blue Letter Bible app or website.

Users can type any word into the search, and Blue Letter Bible will instantly show you every place in the Bible where the word exists.

So test this book. Look up *dunamis, power, gift, Spirit, baptism,* or any other word, phrase, or thought that my book or any book on this topic attempts to teach you. Be like the Bereans and test everything!

In regard to the gifts, do your own Bible study on the gospels and the book of Acts. See how the disciples were taught by Jesus how to use God's dunamis power. Then check out the book of 1 Corinthians chapters 12–14 to learn more about your inheritance. The Bible has page after page demonstrating, communicating, and teaching on these topics. Knowledge is power. The more you know, the less susceptible to false teachings you will become.

Listen to the Lord's Voice

Truth is foundational.

To implement our inheritance, we need to build our lives on the truth of God's word.

Yes, that means the Bible, but it also means actually listening to the voice, the literal word of the Lord.

Jesus said, "My sheep will know my voice" (John 10:27). Hearing the voice of God is one of the most important parts of the training process.

Why?

This is how Jesus modeled using the inheritance.

Jesus lived in perfect relationship with his Father, and obedience was the fruit of that relationship. Jesus listened to the voice and fulfilled the will of his Father. In John 5:19, Jesus said, *"The Son can do nothing by himself, he can only do what he sees his Father doing because whatever the Father does the Son does also."*

Jesus was leaving an example for us to follow, a training regimen for our exercise routine.

We are not called to be rogue agents doing whatever we want with the dunamis power of God. Remember, this power, your inheritance, is explosive and needs to be handled in accordance with the Holy Spirit's instruction.

The Holy Spirit is the one who empowers, leads, guides, directs, and opens the opportunities for us to put his power into practice. No matter who your mentor is, no matter who is discipling you, without the Holy Spirit, you can do nothing of power or importance in the kingdom of God.

Jesus lived, worked, healed, and taught in obedience to his Father's will, and we are called to replicate his example.

"Eye" See a Healing Miracle

While driving home from the gym, I once again heard the voice of the Lord. This time God was telling me that I needed to pray for a man who needed a miracle in his eyes. Very specific and yet very vague at the same time.

What man? Where? And when will I meet him?

I didn't have any answers, just a seed planted by the Spirit that I needed to pray for a man's eyes to be healed.

After arriving at home, I discovered that I didn't have any protein powder for my post-workout shake so I got back in my car and drove to the store.

Now parked in the shopping center, I could see a man sitting at a table in front of the store. He had a metal box for money and a sign asking for donations to support his drug-rehab program.

As I approached the entrance, we made eye contact and the man asks me for a donation. I apologized thinking that I didn't have any cash and continued into the store without engaging in any further conversation.

After purchasing my protein and walking out of the store, I suddenly realized that I did have a couple dollars in my pocket.

As I was preparing to approach the man, God spoke to me again and said, "That's the man needing a miracle in his eyes."

My stomach dropped. *You sure, God?*

No response.

I noticed the man was reading a book while wearing glasses. So, after putting my money in his donation box, I asked what he was reading. He responded, "The Bible."

I was relieved. Mainly because, in theory, him reading the Bible should make my next request less awkward.

After taking a deep breath and trying to choke down the butterflies, I told him, "This might sound crazy, but God asked me to pray specifically for a man who needed a miracle in his eyes and then he highlighted you."

With a deer in the headlights look, the man said, "Okay?"

I then asked if he could read without his glasses.

The man told me that someone had slashed his eye with a knife while in prison and that his right eye was completely blind.

A simple no would have sufficed.

Sliced with a knife? God, are you sure about this?

Usually, such a story would scare the faith right out of me, but since God was the one leading this expedition, I wasn't worried. He called me to pray for this man, so there must be a purpose. I pressed in.

"Can I pray for you?"

"Sure," he said.

I placed my hand on his shoulder, prayed in Jesus's name, and asked him if anything changed.

The man took off his glasses, looked down at his Bible, started to read perfectly aloud, and then began to weep.

I stood there in silence, not yet understanding what had just happened.

With tears streaming down his face, the man told me that he could see out of both eyes perfectly.

I don't know which one of us was more shocked.

He then admitted that he never thought he would see again but was now able to see and read without his glasses.

I lost it.

I literally started to jump up and down, celebrating in front of the store entrance. "God just healed this guy's eyes! God just healed this guy's eyes!"

I'm dancing, and the man is crying. A lady approaches the store completely confused. We make eye contact as I continue to shout, "God just healed this guy's eyes!" She gave me an awkward look and thumbs up as she kept walking into the store.

I didn't care. God literally just did the eye-healing thing from the Bible!

I hugged the guy and ran into the store to share the good news with every person I could find. "You are not going to believe this!"

People thought I was nuts, but the once blind man was walking proof that the dunamis power of God had just exploded, breaking the chains of blindness off his life.

This story doesn't happen without an explosive inheritance, the Holy Spirit speaking, and someone listening to and obeying the voice of the Lord.

What Does God's Voice Sound Like?

I love sharing that story. And nine times out of ten, I'm asked the same question:

"So what does God's voice sound like?"

Well, I can just as easily describe God's voice to you as you can describe the voice or your wife, kids, or boss to me.

However, by spending time with Jesus, you will eventually learn to discern what his voice sounds like. Just as you could pick your spouse or best friend's voice from a crowd, you can discern the Shepherd's voice as well.

If we are going to walk in the explosive power of the Holy Spirit, we need to train ourselves to listen to the voice of the Lord.

How?

I'm glad you asked.

The Secret of King Solomon

King Solomon is one of the most famous characters in the Bible. He was the wisest, wealthiest, and most successful king recorded in the Bible. Kings and queens would travel across the globe to learn from Solomon's wisdom. He also had the distinct privilege of building God's temple.

What was the secret of Solomon's success?

He had a dream.

And in that dream, God said, "Ask what you wish Me to give you" (1 Kings 3:5).

Now we know that God is not a genie, but this sure sounds similar.

In fact, this is your standard "blank check" scenario. God gave Solomon carte blanche to ask him for anything he wanted. Can you imagine?

What would you ask for?

More importantly, what did Solomon ask for?

We read Solomon's response in 1 Kings 3:7–9:

> *Now, LORD my God, you have made your servant king in place of my father David. But I am only a little child and do not know how to carry out my duties. Your servant is here among the people you have chosen, a great people, too numerous to count or number…*

And now for Solomon's request:

> *So give your servant **a discerning heart** to govern your people and to distinguish between right and wrong. For who is able to govern this great people of yours?*

Solomon could have asked for anything: fame, fortune, power, possessions, pleasure, health, anything under heaven. Instead, Solomon asks for a discerning heart to govern the people of God.

We read God's response to Solomon in 1 Kings 3:10–13:

> *The Lord was pleased that Solomon had asked for this. So God said to him, "Since you have asked for*

> *this and not for long life or wealth for yourself, nor have asked for the death of your enemies but for discernment in administering justice, I will do what you have asked. I will give you a wise and discerning heart, so that there will never have been anyone like you, nor will there ever be. Moreover, I will give you what you have not asked for—both wealth and honor—so that in your lifetime you will have no equal among kings."*

So what was Solomon's secret sauce?

A discerning heart.

If you're like me, this doesn't make sense yet.

To fully understand what was so special about Solomon's request, we need to nerd out for a moment and look at the original language used in 1 Kings 3:9.

The Hebrew word used for *discerning* in 1 Kings 3:9 is the word *shama*. This word means "to hear, listen, and obey."

Solomon asked God for a "hearing heart," or a heart that hears from God. Not only that, Solomon wanted an obedient heart, one that would not only hear from God, but a heart that would obey whatever God said.

To hear from God required that Solomon remained in communication with God, that God would continually speak to Solomon.

Solomon was essentially asking for a relationship with God.

And not just any relationship. Let's take another look at the word *shama*.

The word *shama* can mean multiple things as we previously mentioned (to hear, understand, listen, etc.), but there is only one word for obedience in the Hebrew language, and that is the word *shama*.

Solomon was speaking God's love language: relationship and obedience.

Jesus said in John 14:15, "If you love me, you will keep my commandments." In fact, the phrase, "Obedience is better than sacrifice," is woven throughout the word of God (1 Sam. 15:22; Prov. 21:3; Jer. 7:21; Rom. 5:19).

Solomon did not simply want a resource from God; he wanted a relationship with God. In response, God showed Solomon that when you have a relationship with God, you also get all of God's resources as well.

Thus Saith the Lord

So how do we develop a discerning heart, a hearing heart, like Solomon?

The first step is listening to what the Lord has already spoken.

I'm talking about the word of God, the Bible, God's written word. We have a library filled with sixty-six books divided into two volumes full of God's word.

If we want to develop a hearing heart, we need to listen to what God has already said. In so doing, we will discover what God sounds like. Not only that, but we discover his speech patterns.

God seems to speak often about love, forgiveness, caring for the poor, generosity, trusting in God's faithfulness instead of indulging our fears, etc. These repetitive patterns point us to God's purpose for our lives.

Furthermore, as we read how God speaks in the Bible, the better we become at recognizing when he speaks to us through his Spirit. Again, Jesus said, "My sheep will know my voice." The sheep know the voice of the shepherd because they spend so much time around him and have familiarized themselves with what and how he speaks.

Driving home from the gym that day, I knew it was God's voice because I've read the stories of Jesus healing the blind countless times. I have heard the Shepherd's voice speaking specifically about this topic. So when the Holy Spirit asked me to pray for the healing of a man's eyes, that was familiar to me. I've heard it before.

Which brings us to the next principle needed to ignite our inheritance.

Explosive Obedience

As we just learned in our Hebrew lesson, hearing the voice of God requires obedience. James, the brother of Jesus, says it this way: "Do not merely listen to the word, and so deceive yourselves. Do what it says" (James 1:22).

We exercise our ability to hear from God as we put his word into practice.

If I read a passage from the Bible like Matthew 6:14 or Ephesians 4:32 talking about forgiveness, there is no power in that passage unless I actually forgive.

When I hear that God is calling me to love my enemies in Matthew 5:44, but I hold grudges, continue to quarrel with people, and wonder why I'm lacking peace in my life, maybe it's not a "hearing from God" problem.

If you need wisdom and you read James 1:5, *"If any of you lacks wisdom, you should ask God, who gives generously to all without finding fault, and it will be given to you,"* how foolish would it be not to ask God for wisdom? The power comes from the application.

To read God's word without applying the principle is as worthless as an unopened can of paint. Like the Bible, that can of paint can be a great paperweight, but the transformation of the canvas only comes through the application of the paint.

Information without application is completely powerless.

You can hold a stick of dynamite all day, but until you light the wick and throw the stick, it won't fulfill its purpose. We have to hear and apply the word of the Lord for the power of our inheritance to explode.

Ultimately, it doesn't matter how much you know; it matters how you impact others with that information.

I remember spending time with the Lord in preparation to write this book when he impressed something seemingly impossible on my heart. According to the Lord, I was supposed to contact the senior pastor at the largest church in the area and ask him to preach a message on dunamis power and the gifts of God.

Having attended this particular church for many years, I knew they didn't talk about this topic. In fact, at that time, they rarely taught on any topics at all. The lead pastor was an amazing Bible teacher who exposited and exegeted texts, not topics. For him to go rogue and talk on a random topic would be a miracle in and of itself.

After arguing with the Lord about how awkward this conversation could be, I was eventually obedient.

I share this because I want everyone to understand how desperately I need the grace of God every single day. I once heard it said that anything other than instant obedience is instant disobedience. I trust that the sanctification process will get me to the point of instant obedience every time, but I'm not there yet. I praise God that he is infinitely patient.

Anyway, I reached out to the pastor, shared what God put on my heart, and, to my surprise, the pastor preached the message. Then several months later, while in the gym, I met a man who was healed of terminal cancer after that sermon. Not only was he healed, the person who prayed for his healing was new to the prayer ministry and had never been used by God in this way before. The man from the gym explained that when he went up for prayer, the person praying was so nervous at the news that this man was dying of cancer that his hands started to shake. As my gym friend put it, the prayer minister was shaking so badly that he nearly poked him in the eye when trying to apply the anointing oil to his forehead.

After receiving prayer, my friend was examined by four of the top oncologists in the country. It took four of them because the first three couldn't believe that the cancer was gone. This man should have been dead, but God's power killed the cancer instead.

God doesn't need perfect people; he needs obedient people. It's the power of God, not the power of people, that makes the dunamis power so explosive. If we are willing to partner with God, he will bring the boom!

Speaking of explosions, can you imagine knowing the cure for cancer or having the ability to blow up any debilitating disease or demon and not telling anyone about it? What a waste!

How sad if all you do after reading this book is say, "Well, that's nice to hear. I'm glad that God has given me the power to literally live like Jesus and solve any problem plaguing our society. What's new on Netflix?"

Can you see how complacency has the power to close your ears to the voice and purposes of God?

Thankfully, God is gracious and can break through even the most blocked eardrums.

So let's take a moment to exercise those hearing muscles.

What I want you to do right now is stop, put the book down, pick up a pen and some paper, and answer this question: "If God gave me the power to correct any problem currently plaguing society, how would I invest that inheritance?"

What was the first thought that came into your head? Did it sound like something Jesus would have said? Did it involve: feeding the hungry, freeing prisoners, caring for the poor, fighting injustices, or protecting vulnerable people?

That was probably the Holy Spirit.

See, you can hear from God!

Are you discouraged thinking that what you heard could never happen?

Excellent! It's usually God when the problem and solution appears impossible.

Prison Break

Several years ago, I attended the wedding of a classmate with my wife. After the ceremony, we were seated at dinner. This was when God asked me to tell one of my classmates about Jesus. At the time I didn't have the opportunity as this person was at the bridal party table across the courtyard, but the Holy Spirit continued to prompt me throughout the night.

Time quickly slipped away, and I found myself at the end of the evening without having been obedient. It seemed like my opportunity was lost, but as we left the wedding and walked toward our car, I saw my classmate in the distance walking in our direction.

I prayed for the confidence to fulfill God's request because I did not have a relationship with this particular person, and the Holy Spirit responded, "Just tell him that Jesus loves him." That was easy enough.

As we crossed paths, he said good night and I stopped walking. This was the moment. It's now or never. Gathering all of my courage and whispering one last prayer, I said, "Hey, John, while I was sitting at dinner, God asked me to tell you that Jesus loves you."

If you can imagine the worst possible expression on someone's face, that was his response.

"Why would you say that? Do you tell that to everyone? Why would you say that to me?"

In my mind, this was worst-case scenario: an awkward encounter with a combative response. Great.

Completely caught off guard and not at all ready for that response, I replied, "I'm simply being obedient to share what God said. Jesus loves you, John."

"Okay. Thanks," was his reply.

I could tell the conversation was going nowhere, so I said good night, and he turned around to walk away.

It was brutal. But I received a phone call from two of his friends several weeks later. I honestly have no idea how they got my number, but they said, "I don't know what you shared with John at the wedding, but whatever you shared is working."

Not understanding what that meant, I thought, *Did John give his life to Jesus? And why would these guys care?* I knew they weren't Christians.

As it turned out, after high school, John became a heroin addict. His friends and family had tried everything to help him but nothing worked. John was in and out of rehabs and was actively burning bridges with everyone who loved him by lying and stealing. God knew that John was at the end of his rope.

John's friends asked me if I would reach out to him to continue the conversation we started at the wedding. Totally blown away by what was happening, I called John. He had many questions about what happened that night in the parking lot and why I would say that Jesus loved him. John felt completely unworthy of God's love and wanted to understand how anyone could love someone like him. We talked through the gospel of God's grace and prayed together. At the end of the conversation, John asked if we could talk again. Those questions and conversations continued for a few months, but John is now more than five years clean and sober.

Nothing is impossible for our God. No heart is too far from the love of God. Paul said it best: "For I am convinced that neither death nor life, neither angels nor demons, neither the present nor the future, nor any powers, neither height nor depth, nor anything else in all creation, will be able to separate us from the love of God that is in Christ Jesus our Lord" (Rom. 8:38–39).

Little did I know the impact that one simple sentence could have on the human heart. Telling my classmate that Jesus loved him seemed so elementary, but the dunamis power of God snowballed until the momentum broke through his prison walls. John is now a free man.

Never underestimate the dunamis power of God. Some people lose hope when looking at the size of the problem, whether it's an addiction, broken relationship, cancer, or simply stepping out in obedience; but that's the wrong approach. Instead of sizing up the problem, size up the power of God. Is there anything impossible for God?

So if the problem you feel purposed to pursue is bigger than you, pray and ask God for the dunamis power to break down the walls of impossibility.

Ready or Not, Holy Spirit, Come!

Getting back to hearing and obeying, sometimes the instruction from God won't make sense.

For example, God instructed the Israelites to circle the city of Jericho seven times for the fortified walls to fall, Jesus told his followers to fill stone jars with water so he could make wine at a wedding, and the apostle Peter was instructed to step out of a perfectly buoyant boat to walk on water with Jesus.

None of those instructions made sense, but the breakthrough, the miracle, and the dunamis power of God was only displayed through obedience.

Going back to the miracle where Jesus turned water into wine, Mary, the mother of Jesus, told his disciples, "Do whatever he tells you" (John 2:5).

It's really that simple.

If you want to experience your explosive inheritance, if you want to practice the dunamis power of the Holy Spirit, do whatever God tells you.

This is where things get real, risky, and really uncomfortable.

In Uganda, I was on mission with Alissa, my mom, and our church. It was one of the last nights of the trip, and our pastor brought us to a tent church with about one hundred people in attendance.

While standing under the tent, in the sweltering African heat, the Holy Spirit prompted our pastor. He was in the middle of his message when he stopped and said, "The Holy Spirit has revealed to me that there is a great amount of pain among the people tonight. God loves you and wants to relieve your pain through his power."

Without informing the team beforehand, our pastor told the people that we were going to pray and ask the Holy Spirit to highlight those who needed healing.

On the spot, standing in front of the entire church, we were supposed to pray and ask the Holy Spirit who needed healing and where.

I hope my face didn't express the thoughts running through my mind in the moment: *I've never done this before. What if nothing happens?*

Our pastor then began to point people out of the audience and prophetically call out their pains and infirmities. People were responding all over the room, confirming that he was correct. They would then come up to the front for healing prayer.

While he was prophesying, I was praying, like I've never prayed before: "Please, Holy Spirit, show me the pain of your people."

Immediately, I felt a throbbing, nagging pain in my right thumb and right side, simultaneously.

Before praying that prayer, I felt perfectly fine. No pain. Then I asked God to show me the pain of the people, and my body began to experience pain.

Coincidence? Maybe.

God answering my prayer? Most likely.

My pastor paused from prophesying and asked the team if anyone had a word from God.

I stepped forward, completely out of my comfort zone, and said, "As I prayed, I felt pain in my right thumb and side. I believe there is someone here with the same pain. If that's you, please come up for—"

Before I could finish, a middle-aged African woman in the center of the tent jumped out of her chair began waving her arms to identify herself, and with tears streaming down her face, she approached the altar.

The expectant faith of this woman amazed me. She did not believe that this was some coincidence; she knew it was God.

We prayed, and God responded.

The woman then reported no pain.

The now healed woman hugged me and returned to her seat.

Did I hear the audible voice of the Lord? No.

Did he communicate through a feeling in my body? Yes.

What am I saying?

We cannot afford to put God in a box.

Just because we haven't heard, read, or seen God do something before does not establish a limitation for him.

Nothing is impossible for our God.

One thing my pastor always teaches the mission team is, "Never look surprised at anything you see in ministry." He knew we would see and experience the impossible and wanted this to be normal.

Knowing our God, what he has already done and has promised to do, we should never be surprised by the impossible. He is the God who spoke the universe into existence. He is the God who split the Red Sea. He is the God who laid down his life after being nailed to a tree. He is the God who defeated death and walked out of the grave to give us eternal life.

Don't be surprised when you hear, feel, see, or experience the impossible or unfamiliar when following him.

So if you want to exercise your inheritance, listen to the Holy Spirit, no matter what he says. It doesn't have to make sense, it doesn't need to be comfortable; it just needs to be done.

A Sign at 702

Throughout this chapter on exercising your inheritance, there has been a major focus on listening to the voice of the Lord.

This is important because listening to and obeying the LORD was the example that Jesus left us to follow.

Throughout his ministry, Jesus said that he only does and says what he sees and hears from his Father (John 5:19–20, John 8:28, John 12:49).

Jesus then ascended to heaven to send us the Holy Spirit. When describing the Spirit of God, Jesus said that "he will not speak on his own authority, but whatever he hears he will speak" (John 16:13). This sounds a lot like Jesus's relationship to the Father.

Since Jesus is the one who left us instructions about our inheritance, it's important that we put his words and example into practice.

Well, what happens if we aren't sure we are hearing the Holy Spirit? Maybe it's our own internal dialogue or the pizza we ate last night. How can we discern the difference?

I remember one weekend where I received two separate invitations to play in poker tournaments at conflicting times on the same day.

Before starting my Bible study on the morning of the card tournaments, I made up my mind to play at the game in Livermore instead of the one in Castro Valley.

As I spent time with the Lord in prayer, I kept hearing the name Castro Valley repeated over and over again in my head.

Not sure if this was God or my own subconscious dialogue, I asked him for confirmation, "Is this you, Lord? If so, can you make it clear?"

The number 702 immediately popped into my mind. Just like the name Castro Valley, the number 702 pulsated again and again.

I thought, *Seven hundred two? What does that mean?*

Then the concept of time came into mind, so I said, "Okay, Lord, if you want me to play cards in Castro Valley instead of Livermore, let it be 7:02 a.m. right now."

I looked at my phone, and it was exactly 7:02 a.m.

God must have a sense of humor.

Suffice it to say, I changed my plans to play in Castro Valley that day.

Believe it or not, I went to the tournament, took first place for a nice payout, and left the club thanking God for bringing me there.

Something wasn't right though.

God wouldn't have just brought me here so I could win money, would he?

Did I miss his purpose in bringing me to this place?

As I reached my car, I also realized that I forgot my keys inside the club.

Turning around, I headed inside.

Almost everyone had left the card room except the woman who was in charge of the game. I hadn't spoken much to her during the tournament, but I now had an unobstructed opportunity to share the gospel with her.

After a bit of small talk, I shared about Jesus. Then I noticed that she had a cane sitting next to her, so I inquired about her condition. She revealed having severe arthritis in her back and knees. I asked how badly the pain bothered her and said it was a ten out of ten on the pain scale.

The women let me pray for her in Jesus name, and when I finished praying, she had a look on her face that said, "What the heck did you just do to me?"

I asked if anything changed during the prayer, and she reported that the once-tormenting pain was now gone.

Bingo!

Yahtzee!

Winner, winner, chicken dinner!

God did it again!

The Lord loved this woman so much that he brought someone to her card game to share the gospel and set her free from a debilitating condition.

To Fleece or Not to Fleece

Now I prefaced the last story with the purpose of answering, "What should we do when we don't know if it's the Lord?"

Ask for clarification.

Questioning doesn't disqualify your faith.

We see this in the life of Gideon from Judges chapter 6. This story takes place during a time when Israel lived in rebellion against the Lord.

While the Israelites were in rebellion against the Lord, a group of raiders known as the Midianites ravaged the land of Israel. The Midianites set fire to the fields of Israel, burning their food supply, while also killing all the cattle and other livestock.

The Israelites were so afraid of the Midianites that they left their homes to live in the caves of the surrounding mountains.

While in hiding, the Israelites cried out to the Lord for deliverance from their oppressors and God responded by calling a man named Gideon from the tribe of Manasseh.

God approached Gideon and said that he was chosen to deliver his people from the hand of the Midianites, but Gideon wasn't sure that he was hearing from God.

Three times Gideon asked God for a sign to show him that he was hearing from the Lord, and three times God gave Gideon an affirmative answer.

Godly dads don't get mad when their kids ask questions.

Does Gideon display a lack of faith in the Lord? Sure.

Is God's grace sufficient to overcome his questions? Absolutely.

After receiving his three requested confirmations, Gideon led a three hundred-man army to defeat the Midianites through the dunamis power of God.

The Bible says in Judges 7:22 that the Lord caused the men in the Midianite army to turn on each other with their swords. After slaughtering one another, the remaining men of Midian fled from the Israelites and were eventually all captured and killed.

Through the miraculous power of God, Gideon led the Israelites to victory resulting in forty years of peace through the land.

God can handle your questions.

If you don't know or understand, ask.

His answers aren't always immediate like in Gideon's case, but God is faithful.

Ask and then exercise patience by waiting on the Lord for his reply.

Increased Intensity Training

When talking about exercise, it's important to point out a principle that we see in the life of Peter Parker and anyone competently training to build muscle size, strength, or endurance.

When Peter realized that he had new power, he gradually began to test the limits of possibility. Before he swings from a single skyscraper, Peter started out on a much smaller scale. From rooftops to trees to towers, to the tallest buildings in New York City, Peter implemented the principle of progressive overload.

The same is true when training to transform your body. To increase muscular size, strength, or endurance, you must continually increase one of two things: weight or volume. By increasing the amount lifted or the number of repetitions, your body is forced to adapt, change, and grow.

Progressive overload trains the body to constantly push beyond limits, crush comfort levels, and blast past plateaus. If you continue to do the same thing over and over again without challenging your body, it won't grow and you'll eventually become complacent.

Faith is no different. It's a muscle that needs to grow. That is why God uses the principle of progressive overload to develop dunamis power in his people.

Being asked to stand in front of a crowd in Africa and pray to know the pain of the people who were expecting God to heal them wasn't easy. In fact, I don't think there has ever been a time when God's "ask" was easy. If it were, it wouldn't require faith. But God had been progressively building my faith getting me to that point.

How did God train me? By consistently showing me his faithfulness both throughout the history of our relationship and by reading "His Story," the Bible. And to specifically exercise my faith, God has progressively grown me in the area of giving.

Since Alissa and I first married, God has continually challenged us to give more, with each "ask" increasing with intensity.

I remember returning from our honeymoon to the reality that I was the only one working and we had huge debts to pay.

We can joke about it now, but Alissa and I both brought baggage into our marriage. I brought a BC "Before Christ" history of sexual promiscuity; and Alissa, the pure virgin lamb, brought a mountain of college debt the size of many American mortgages.

Heaping insult to injury, Alissa's college loan payments were now due and we didn't even have the money to pay our basic bills.

Literally, our first real marriage conversation confronted the fact that we would be in the red next month unless Alissa got a job. That is not the conversation anyone wants to have after a romantic honeymoon in Hawaii.

So we show up to church that Sunday looking for some relief, and instead, the pastor informs us that the Lord wanted to grow the church in their giving.

Then the pastor asked everyone to pray.

Specifically, we were asked to pray that the Holy Spirit would show us how much we were supposed to give, above and beyond our tithe for the next two years.

Honestly, I felt relieved because I knew, that God knew, there was no way we could afford to give more than our tithe at that time. I looked around the room thinking, *Sucks for you guys, we've got a hard pass on this one.*

But we were obedient and prayed anyway.

I guess I didn't know God that well.

Immediately, the Holy Spirit spoke and gave us a number.

And not a small number either. It was a number that seemed simply irresponsible.

I remember thinking,

God.

Come on.

It's me, Matt.

You know me.

You know our situation.

You know we can't afford that.

What are you doing?

That number was burned in my brain all week. I couldn't shake it. The more I prayed, the more it resonated.

God's "ask" didn't make sense.

It was uncomfortable. It was risky.

It was the word of the Lord.

Despite our doubts, Alissa and I agreed to obey and give God what he asked.

That Sunday we wrote our first check.

I can't call it an act of faith because there were moments when we felt like we were drowning in our doubts and our debts. Instead, it was more like desperate hope. It was a hope that cried out, "God, you have got to come through. We are depending on you. You are our only hope!"

I don't know that I've hoped so hard in my life. Yet, despite our doubts, God answered.

The next week, to our amazement, Alissa landed a job.

Shortly after that I received an additional source of income.

Then someone randomly paid off our remaining car loan.

During those two years, Alissa and I both received raises and bonuses. We were allowed to work overtime. I even got a huge promotion at work. The blessings just kept pouring in. It was overwhelming.

After the two years, we paid off Alissa's six-figure loan and became completely debt free.

I could write a book about God's economy and his incredible generosity, but I'll leave it here, our breakthrough came on the other side of our obedience.

Please note that the breakthrough is not always financial. I'm not preaching a prosperity gospel here, but God does honor his principles.

Even if God never gave anyone anything else other than Jesus, we would be the wealthiest people to ever walk the planet but God does bless obedience (Eph. 6:1–3; Deut. 5:16; Isa. 1:19; Rom. 2:13; John 9:31; Deut. 30:9–10). He is our inheritance and reward. We have every spiritual blessing in Christ (Eph. 1:3), and "The Lord is my shepherd, I lack nothing" (Ps. 23:1).

The purpose of me sharing this portion of my life was to show that, yes, God is generous and honors faith but also that faith requires obedience and is often risky.

Ever since God's first financial "ask," the amount has only ever increased. We were actually asked to exponentially increase the amount and duration of that first gift. After the two years, we were asked to double the amount of money for four years, then double the amount again for eight years, and so on.

A Malawi-Owie

I remember raising money for a mission trip so Alissa and I could serve the Lord by sharing the gospel in Romania. We hosted a successful fundraiser and brought the cash to church that Sunday to make our mission trip payment.

Well, that Sunday we had a special guest speaker that our church supported on the mission field in Malawi. After sharing her missionary field report and all the testimonies of God's faithfulness, our pastor asked the congregation to bless this woman. Again, he asked us to pray and ask God how much to give her.

We prayed, and God said, "All of it."

All of it? What do you mean "All of it"?

"The money from your mission trip fundraiser is for her. I'll take care of you," God replied.

I started to sweat.

That was a lot of money.

We needed that money!

We put a ton off effort into our fundraiser. Is God really asking us to give it all away?

He was.

And we did.

All of it, to the missionary.

We now had nothing for our mission trip, but God is faithful. Check this out.

When I was wrestling about this decision, and trust me when I say that I wrestled with this one, God gave me an assurance.

God reminded me of his promise in Matthew 19:29 when Jesus said, *"Everyone who has left houses or brothers or sisters or father or mother or wife or children or fields for my sake will receive a hundred times as much and will inherit eternal life."*

Strangely enough, when God quoted the verse to me, instead of saying, "A hundred times," he said, "Tenfold." This wasn't in the Bible, but it was the word of God. And guess what, for the first time in our lives, Alissa got a bonus. Do you know how much that bonus was?

Ten times what we gave.

God is faithful, Amen!

I started out this section sharing that God's "asks" aren't easy, but through obedience, they are blessed. Well, like I said, since those first two major financial tests, the "asks" have only gotten bigger. I'm literally talking two, three, five, and ten times bigger. Each ask more challenging than the previous one, but each act of obedience led to an explosive breakthrough in our lives and the lives of others.

If you want to grow in dunamis power, exercise the principle of progressive overload:

Spend increasingly more time in prayer, reading the Word, fasting, serving, giving, taking risks, using your gifts.

Also, like any effective fitness plan, set goals, establish a routine, and track your progress.

If your goal is to see people get healed, implement a routine of regularly praying for people. Whenever you see a need, pray.

Ask God what he is calling you to do.

Also, pray for yourself. Ask for boldness. Pray for the compassion of Jesus. Compassion is what compelled Jesus to heal people and work miracles (Matt. 14:14, 15:32, 20:34).

Pray for the compassion of Christ to compel you to pray for people publicly. It may feel uncomfortable at first, but so does any new exercise routine. Eventually, praying for people will become so routine that the pain and discomfort you once experienced won't even register.

Finally, track your progress.

I've found that journaling or keeping a note in your phone of all the prayers, answers, praises, and testimonies provides a beautiful history and helpful accountability. When you face another situation needing the explosive power of your inheritance, you have a written record to review of all the times that God came through.

The more you exercise the muscles of your faith and put the power into practice, the stronger they get.

Remember, *"Physical training is good, but training for godliness is much better, promising benefits in this life and in the life to come"* (1 Tim. 4:8).

Train to share your testimony.

Train to listen to the Lord.

Train to share the gospel.

Train to pray.

Train to prophesy.

Train to give.

Train to put your gifts into practice.

Ultimately, it's not about trying, it's about training.

A Perceived Impediment

Earlier, I mentioned receiving the gift of tongues after nearly seven years of asking and pursuing God in prayer.

Well, after receiving this gift at the Grand Canyon, I wasn't even sure that it was real because it sounded so elementary.

In fact, I only had one word, *Dada*.

Yes, *Dada*, like a baby would say.

It was actually a little embarrassing at first because all I could do over and over again was repeat this baby babel, which is why I didn't tell anyone about my Grand Canyon experience.

I remember asking God in our hotel room if what I received was real.

God said, "What is a baby's first word?"

Well, typically, its *Dada* or *Mama*.

"And who gave you that gift?" he replied.

It finally hit me.

My Heavenly Father gave me a new language that needed to be developed.

So I started practicing.

Every day I would put into practice what God had given me while asking the Holy Spirit to increase it.

Over time, my vocabulary grew.

I even implemented the principle of progressive overload by speaking this new language for an increased amount of time every day. My spiritual workout plan included a training session that would increase by one minute each time.

I still practice this gift today and enjoy myself in the process. Remember, the gift of tongues is the only one intended for personal edification (1 Cor. 14:4). Pursue it, practice it, and enjoy it.

God gives the best gifts!

Mixing Business with Pleasure

Speaking of gifts, let's go back to the story of Solomon for a second.

Recall his request from 1 Kings 3.

Solomon asked for a discerning heart to lead the people of the Lord.

In return, Solomon not only received his request, God gave him all the resources he would need to lead God's people well. God gave him the wisdom, wealth, and health to accomplish the Father's will.

What I find interesting is that God was prepared to grant Solomon anything he requested.

As God pointed out, Solomon could have asked for wealth, long life, or the death of his enemies but he didn't. Instead, Solomon asked for something that would sustain his inheritance.

Solomon inherited the kingdom of Israel from his father, David, but these were God's people who Solomon was entrusted to lead. He needed God's help to succeed like his father, David, did.

Since Solomon sought something close to God's heart, the success of God's kingdom, Solomon was given everything he needed to succeed.

Sound familiar?

On the Sermon on the Mount, the most famous sermon that Jesus ever gave, he addressed many things including worry, lack, and fear. Jesus specifically told his followers not to worry about their lives, what they would eat, drink, or wear. Instead, Jesus said, "Seek first the kingdom of God and his righteousness, and all these things will be added to you as well" (Matt. 6:33).

Jesus was teaching the principle that God demonstrated in the life of King Solomon. Not only that, Jesus was communicating the consistency of God's faithfulness. God is the still the same today as he was in Solomon's day and will continue to be the same throughout eternity.

Why is this important?

The same God who gifted Solomon with the resources to build God's kingdom is the same God and the same resources he has made available to us to do the same thing!

Like the story of Solomon, Jesus was teaching that when we pursue God's passions, when we pursue his priorities, when we pursue the purposes of God, his perfect provision follows.

Pursue the Passion

The story of Solomon provides the perfect introduction to another principle needed to ignite our inheritance.

But first, let's take a quick trip down memory lane to set the stage.

Growing up in California I have some amazing memories snowboarding around Lake Tahoe. Ever since my first trip to Alpine Meadows in middle school, I fell in love with the sport and snowboarding became my passion.

Thankfully, we had some amazing family friends who owned a cabin in South Lake Tahoe. These friends also happened to work at the best resort in Tahoe and regularly blessed us with free lift tickets.

My dad was not into snow sports, but he still gifted me with some new equipment on Christmas because he knew that I was passionate about snowboarding. Instead of snowboarding, my dad was passionate about golf. So for Father's Day, my wife and I took my dad golfing. We ended up enjoying the experience so much that Alissa and I golfed almost every other weekend for the rest of the year.

My dad took notice of our newfound passion for golf and began to gift us with all the equipment we needed to excel in the sport he loved. These gifts didn't arrive on special occasions like Christmas or my birthday but randomly as an expression of my dad's excitement that we were pursuing his passions.

When we became passionate about my dad's passions, he provided everything we needed to succeed: clubs, bags, balls, tees, clothes, green fees…he even offered to give us lessons.

If this is what our earthly father's will do when we align our passions with theirs, what will our Heavenly Father do?

Better yet, how can we even know what our Heavenly Father is passionate about?

For that matter, how can we know what anyone is passionate about?

The answer, my friends, is simple.

Follow their resources.

When you look at my dad's bank statement, you can track his purchases. Follow the trail of his finances and you'll find his passions. And it is clear by looking at my dad's bank statement that the guy loves to golf.

God, on the other hand, has unlimited resources; but if you look at his ledger, you'll find that he poured out his most precious resource to purchase people.

God's most-prized possession is his Son Jesus, and God willingly allowed his Son to die as a substitutionary sacrifice to save people.

That's right. God sacrificed his Son to pay the penalty for our sins.

God so loved the world, he so wanted our relationship to be reconciled, that he bought our freedom with the blood of his only begotten Son.

Since God poured out his most precious resource to purchase people, we can confidently conclude that God's passion is people.

The passion of the Christ was all about people.

God loves people!

Not just people, God loves you, specifically and individually.

I love the thought that if you were the only person on earth, Jesus would have still gone to the cross for you. You were worth the excruciating torture that Jesus suffered.

"For God so loved the world that he gave his one and only Son, that whoever believes in him shall not perish but have everlasting life" (John 3:16).

To ignite your inheritance, follow me into the next section to discover "the principle of purpose."

The Purpose of Passion

Purpose is a weighty topic.

Some people often spend their whole lives bogged down and burdened by the thought of purpose.

What is the purpose of life? Will I ever find it? If I do, will I ever fulfill it? Not able to find answers to those questions, many people consequently live in fear of their purpose.

If that's you, I've got some good news!

Just as God has an incredible inheritance for you, he also planted purpose in you. That's why Jesus said, *"Come to me, all you who are weary and burdened and I will give you rest. Take my yoke upon you and learn from me, for I am gentle and humble in heart, and you will find rest for your souls. For my yoke is easy and my burden is light" (Matt. 11:28–30).* In other words, there is no need to fear your God-given purpose.

Very simply put, the purpose of life is to enjoy relationship with God and help others do the same. This makes sense when considering that the God of the Bible is relational, not religious. He doesn't want religion stealing what his relationship came to restore.

Think about this.

In relationship, intimacy increases when we invest in and pursue our partner's passions.

I'm learning this through my marriage. When I invest in the interests of my wife, our intimacy increases.

Simple as that.

By pursuing Alissa's passions for bowling, country music, puzzles, *Sister Act*, or Whitney Houston, I express a vested interest in our intimacy by communicating, "What you value is valuable to me because I value you."

God works the same way.

When we pursue his passions, our intimacy increases and we fulfill our purpose.

In summary, let's work out a little logic:

If our purpose is to enjoy intimacy with God...

And to accomplish that purpose includes pursuing God's passions...

And God's passion is people...

Then we can confidently conclude that our purpose includes pursuing people.

Pursue people with what? The gospel, the gifts, the dunamis power and love of God! Our explosive inheritance has the power to reconcile people back to God. That's why we are called God's ambassadors who communicate a message of reconciliation to the world (2 Cor. 5). We get to participate in God's plan of reconciliation as "Co laborers with Christ" (1 Cor. 3:9)!

How?

By pursuing people through our passions!

Did you catch that?

God wants to partner with you through your passions to pursue his.

Just as I am able to pursue a deeper relationship with my dad through golf, we too can pursue a deeper relationship with God through our passions.

Let me explain.

Fishin' for a Mission

After Jesus arrives on the scene, he starts to build his ministry team.

The first disciples that Jesus pursues were Andrew and Peter. These brothers were enjoying their passion for fishing when Jesus approached them and extended the greatest invitation in human history: "*Follow me and I'll make you fishers of men*" (Matt. 4:19).

Jesus took fishing, the passion of his disciples, aligned it with his passion for people, and turned "fishing for people" into their purpose.

This is the sweet spot: when our passions align with God's purposes.

What does this look like practically?

Great question!

I am passionate about snowboarding.

There are people on the lifts, in the lodges, and all around the mountain.

God is passionate about those people.

I can pursue people with the gospel of God's love and grace while enjoying my passion for snowboarding.

I am also passionate about fitness and exercise.

There are people at the gym.

God loves those people.

By pursuing people through my passion for fitness, enjoying the gym has become part of my purpose.

How awesome is that?

Whatever you are passionate about, exercise it! Because God wants to use your passion for business, travel, knitting, shopping, food, or whatever it is that you find fun to fulfill your purpose.

Promise of Provision

The greatest part about this is God promises to provide for all of your needs when your passions align with his.

Like my dad providing all the necessary golf equipment, if your purpose is to reach people with the gospel, God will gift you everything you need to succeed: all the plans, finances, power, opportunity, confidence, connections, etc.

Your explosive inheritance is an inexhaustible resource.

When we seek the things of God, when we look to expand his kingdom, exalt his name, build his body, when we are passionate about his purposes, God equips us and provides everything we need.

Paul shares the following promise in Philippians 4:19: "My God will meet all of your needs according to his glorious riches in Christ Jesus."

Just take a look at the lives of Jesus's disciples. They followed Jesus, pursued people, and never once did they lack anything. All of their needs were constantly provided for. The entire gospel account from Matthew 1 to John 21 demonstrates the truth that God provides for all of our needs when we pursue his passions.

So let's get practical.

As we continue to exercise our inheritance, there is one final piece of training we need to practice before approaching the employment phase of the Peter Parker Process. As disciples of Jesus with dunamis power, we need to learn how to think with the Power Approach.

The Power Approach

I'm sure we can all think of examples when Christians have pursued people with the gospel using a powerless or ineffective approach. Many of us have seen guilt, shame, judgment, condemnation, megaphones, and signs used to propel people away from God when the intention was to bring them the gospel.

The truth is, even with good intentions, the wrong approach can be a stumbling block instead of a stepping-stone. We want to propel people into the loving arms of our Father, not prevent them from entering his family. Thankfully, Jesus provided us with a training manual in John chapter 13 on how to powerfully pursue people with his mindset that I call the Power Approach.

A little context on this chapter, Jesus is eating the infamous Last Supper with his disciples as he prepares for the cross. This is the last meal before Jesus provides a way for all people to be reconciled to God through his death and resurrection. But before that, Jesus models a mindset.

Let's pick up the story in John 13:1: *"It was just before the Passover Festival. Jesus knew that the hour had come for him to leave this world and go to the Father. Having loved his own who were in the world, he loved them to the end. The evening meal was in progress, and the devil had already prompted Judas, the son of Simon Iscariot, to betray Jesus."*

Now pay attention, don't miss this!

John 13:3 is the power approach for pursing people: *"Jesus knew that the Father had given him authority over everything and that he had come from God and would return to God."*

The mindset that Jesus modeled to properly pursue people incorporated his authority, history, and destiny.

Jesus then took this mindset, humbled himself, and washed the feet of his disciples. Remember, almost all of these men would either betray, deny, or abandon Jesus in the next twenty-four hours. Jesus knew this and loved them anyway. Jesus had his authority, history, and destiny in mind. We must do the same.

To see the Power Approach in action, let's go to the graveyard in Mark chapter 5.

The Author's Authority

Right before this section of scripture, Jesus preached his most famous Sermon on the Mount. After preaching, Jesus leaves the multitudes of people behind on the hill to demonstrate to his disciples the truth found in 1 Corinthians 4:20: "That the kingdom of God is not just a matter of words, but of power and authority."

As Jesus comes down from the mountain, he encounters a man with leprosy and heals him, then he heals a centurion's servant, and then Peter's mother-in-law.

Through healing, Jesus demonstrated his authority over the human body.

Then Jesus climbed into a boat with his disciples to sail across a sea. While sailing, the disciples encountered a storm as Jesus was sleeping in the stern. When they woke Jesus, he stopped the storm with a simple command.

Quick recap: before the beginning of Mark 5, Jesus preached the Sermon on the Mount and demonstrated his authority over the human body, wind, and the waves but Jesus wasn't finished. We pick up the story in Mark 5 when Jesus arrives on the shore across the sea: *"They went across the lake to the region of the Gerasenes. When Jesus got out of the boat, he was met by a man who lived in the cemetery" (Mark 5:1).*

The moment Jesus arrives, he is met by a man. Let me clarify something here. This man was living in the cemetery but did not own a home in the cemetery. He was not employed by the cemetery. He was ostracized, secluded, and abandoned to live among the dead as defiled and unclean. Why?

Between the three gospel accounts in Matthew, Mark, and Luke, the "man of the tombs" was described as violent, naked, homeless, and full of demons. The Bible says that no one could subdue, restrain, or bind him with chains.

I'm not sure which factor prevented people from binding him. For me it would have been the fact that he was naked. I'm not binding naked dudes with anything: chains, rope, handcuffs, nothing. We all have boundaries. That's where I draw mine, but maybe that's a topic for another book. I digress…

Anyway, Mark 5 tells us that when people were finally able to chain him, he was so strong that he snapped the chains and broke free. And the guy clearly had help because when Jesus asked for his name, Legion was the answer because he had many demons living in him.

We are also told that this man was suffering: *"Night and day among the tombs and in the hills he would cry out and cut himself with stones" (Mark 5:5).*

Why is this important? For those who have never heard this story before, I'm going to spoil the ending. Jesus took the Power Approach to pursue one person. Knowing that this man was suffering, Jesus sailed across a stormy sea to set him free. That's our God. If there was only one person on the planet, he would have still gone to the cross. God loves us that much.

I believe someone reading this book needs to know that God hears your cries and collects your tears. They are precious to him. God is incredibly compassionate when it comes to his kids. God sees you! You are not forgotten. He has brought you to this book to tell you that he is in pursuit of your heart.

If you are suffering right now, Jesus cares. If you are hurting, this message is for you: God loves you and is pursuing you. Jesus literally went through hell and high water to pursue this one man, and he has done the same for you.

Getting back to the walking-dead demonized man, we read: *"When he saw Jesus from a distance, he ran and fell on his knees in front of him" (Mark 5:6).*

Don't miss this. A man, full of demons, runs to Jesus and falls on his knees in front of him. This is a picture of submission to Jesus's authority. Many of you know how the story plays out. Jesus delivers the man from the demons and sends them into a herd of pigs, which then run off a cliff and drown.

In all the gospels, you will never find a storm Jesus couldn't stop, an illness he couldn't heal, a demonized person he couldn't deliver, a sin he couldn't forgive, or a life he couldn't redeem. Jesus has a perfect track record with his Power Approach.

I'm writing to tell somebody, when you, like the man of the tombs, humble yourself before the Lord and submit to his authority, Jesus will show himself faithful to forgive, heal, deliver, save, redeem, reconcile, and restore anything in your life. If you believe that, right where you are reading, give God some praise. He is worthy.

As we have just read, Jesus has now demonstrated his authority over the human body, the weather, and the spirit realm. Even demons submitted to Jesus authority.

Jesus pursued people, relieved their suffering, and delivered them from demonic oppression and possession all with his authority and power approach.

As followers and disciples of Jesus, this is our model and we have been called, commissioned, and commanded to do the same. And yes, through the Holy Spirit, we have been given the authority of Jesus to pursue people with his power.

You have authority.

Your prayers have authority.

You know how I know that?

I was recently reminded by a man that I had never met before that I should be dead. Through a prophetic word of knowledge, this man said that I was supposed to have died from a drug overdose in college. Not just on one occasion either, there were many times I should not have survived.

God told this man that the prayers of the people around me moved God's heart to have mercy. My life was spared because the power and authority of prayer. You have authority in your prayers to bring your loved ones from death to life.

Mark 5 is my story. My life is living proof that God can take someone addicted, afflicted, depressed, and spiritually dead and resurrect them to new life.

You have this authority (Luke 10:19, 9:1; Matt. 16:15–19; Mark 16:17–18).

If you want to pursue people for God's glory, remember that he has given you the authority!

Going back to John 13, we recall that Jesus had a Power Approach that included his authority, history, and destiny.

This is an all-inclusive package, not an à la carte menu.

Authority without history can be dangerous. Let me explain.

A History of Horror

Forget all the horror movies and scary shows you have ever seen, there is nothing more frightening than a Christian who forgets their history.

If you have ever watched AMC's *The Walking Dead*, or any other zombie movie, you are quite familiar with the fact that zombies eat human flesh. By definition, zombies are walking dead creatures who, by nature, are driven by their desire for flesh. In other words, zombies eat people. That's who they are and what they do.

It should be no surprise to people watching a zombie movie when the zombie starts eating someone's face off. It's zombie nature.

Just as it is ridiculous to become surprised when zombies act according to their nature, it is just as ridiculous when Christians are surprised by and judge those who are acting according to their nature. What nature am I referring to?

According to the word of God, *"As for you, you were dead in your transgressions and sins, in which you used to live when you followed the ways of this world and of the ruler of the kingdom of the air, the spirit who is now at work in those who are disobedient. All of us also lived among them at one time, gratifying the cravings of our flesh and following its desires and thoughts. Like the rest, we were by nature deserving of wrath"* (Eph. 2:1–3 NIV).

Notice this section of scripture uses a lot of past-tense verbiage. Why? It's inclusive in nature, meaning that we can all identify.

"You were" means that in your past. This description applied to you as well. Meaning, you do not get a pass here. Understand that Ephesians 2 was once you as well. Like the man of the tombs, we too were living in the cemetery controlled by our sinful nature.

Let me be a little more direct: Colossians 2:13 says, "You were dead because of your sins."

I would like to propose a question:

Are there variations of dead?

By variation, I mean degree. Can one person be more dead than another?

Ephesians and Colossians 2 tell us that we were spiritually dead because of our sins. All of us. We were all once spiritually dead living according to our desires for the flesh.

Ephesians 2 seems to say that all of us we were once like zombies, dead and driven by our desire for the flesh.

Now we know that "flesh" in this context, does not mean that we enjoyed eating people? To be "driven by our desire for the flesh" means that we were driven by our sinful human nature.

What's my point? It should be no surprise when people who are not following Jesus are not acting like Jesus. They are simply acting according to their fallen sinful nature. It is human nature to fall short of God's glorious standard (Rom. 3:23).

Let me take this a step further.

Romans chapter 1 is a famous chapter that Christians have historically used to point out the flaws and sins of other people. Romans 1 goes like this:

> They (meaning sinners) are full of envy, murder, strife, deceit and malice. They are gossips, slanderers, God-haters, insolent, arrogant and boastful; they invent ways of doing evil; they disobey their parents; they have no understanding, no fidelity, no love, no mercy. Although they know God's righteous decree that those who do such things deserve death, they not only continue to do these very things but also approve of those who practice them. (Rom. 1:28–32 NIV)

The danger of this section of scripture occurs when we fail to read the very next chapter. Romans 2 says this:

> You, therefore, have no excuse, you who pass judgment on someone else, for at whatever point you judge another, you are condemning yourself, because you who pass judgment do the same things. Now we know that God's judgment

against those who do such things is based on truth. So when you, a mere human being, pass judgment on them and yet do the same things, do you think you will escape God's judgment? (Rom. 2:1–3 NIV)

Jesus had every right to judge and condemn the Mark 5 man of the tombs, but he didn't. Instead, Jesus said, "I have not come to condemn the world, but so save it" and "it's not the healthy who need a doctor, but the sick" (John 3:17; Luke 5:31).

If we want to pursue people with the love of Jesus, we have got to remember where we came from.

We too were like the man of the tombs. "For all have sinned and have fallen short of Gods glory" (Rom. 3:5). That includes me, and it includes you. But the good news is that our story does not stop in the graveyard.

We worship the God who resurrected from the dead and got out of the grave so that he could bring us from death to life as well, "because of his great love for us, God, who is rich in mercy, made us alive in Christ even when we were dead in our transgressions, it is by grace you have been saved. It is a gift from God, not by works, so that no one can boast" (Eph. 2:4)

Bottom-line, if we want to pursue people with a Power Approach, we have to remember our history.

The Destination of Destiny

After the man of the tombs submitted to Jesus's authority and was delivered, the people of the town found this man "*dressed, in his right mind, and sitting at Jesus feet*" (Mark 5:15). Then the man who had just been healed, saved, set free, and delivered asked to follow Jesus on his journey across the sea. Why? Because saved people save people, healed people heal people, freed people free people, delivered people deliver people, and revived people revive people.

However, to all of our surprise, Jesus said no. Instead, he ordered that the man return to his family and tell everyone what God had done for him.

Jesus brought wholeness to this man. Remember, due to the demons, this man lost all contact with his community. Not only did he go from death to life, but Jesus was also going to restore the relationships in this man's family. Consequently, Jesus said no to his request.

While the man wanted to reach others, Jesus sent him home to his brothers. The man wanted to reach the nations, but Jesus sent him home to his neighbors. This was his destiny: to share what God had done in his life with people who knew his history.

Jesus took the Power Approach and successfully pursued this man by recognizing his destiny. There is also a promise from God through the Power Approach. If you, like the man of tombs, submit your history under Jesus authority, he will deliver you into your divine destiny.

What do I mean by destiny?

Looking back at John 13 and Jesus's Power Approach, we read, "Jesus *knew that he was returning to the Father*" (John 13:1). Returning to his Father, was Jesus's final destination or destiny. Jesus also predestined his people to follow him to his final destination (Eph. 1:4–5, 11; Rom. 8:29; John 15:16; John 6:44; 2 Tim. 1:9).

In the verses that follow, Jesus is seen washing his disciples' feet. All of them, including Judas and Peter! All of Jesus's disciples were about to abandon, deny, or betray Jesus; but he washed their feet anyway. Why?

Jesus washed the feet of his disciples according to the destiny that his authority afforded them. How? He looked ahead at the grace that was about to be poured out on all of them through the blood he would spill on the cross, and this grace enabled Jesus to love and serve those who didn't deserve it.

Jesus's disciples had destiny on their lives. He knew that they would be the ones to share his good news with the world. Through the Power Approach, Jesus was able to look past their present and into their predestined future. Like Jesus, we are also called to look past the present and see the destiny that God designed for the people in our presence.

Remember the destiny that Jesus designed for the lost, lonely, broken, oppressed, possessed, addicted, and afflicted. Remember that Jesus's history affords us the authority to direct people into their destiny. By exercising this Power Approach, we will lead people out of the graveyard and into their heavenly inheritance!

As we are about to see, we have not only been entrusted with an inheritance, but also a responsibility. As Christ followers, we have all been called, commissioned, and commanded to follow in the footsteps of Jesus by pursuing people with the gospel, making disciples of all nations, destroying the work of the devil, and building the body of Christ.

In other words, we have a job to do!

Let's check out our job description in the employment phase of the Peter Parker Process.

CHAPTER 7

Peter Parker Process
Phase 4: Employ

Fun fact: every superhero, no matter how powerful or well-equipped is employed with the same generic job description. It doesn't matter if you are Spider-Man, Superman, Batman, Ant-Man, or Thor, the job description is the same: to protect and serve, heal and restore, save and deliver, and bring justice to the bad guys.

Different superheroes, same job description.

As it turns out, comics aren't that creative. In fact, they stole the job description right out of God's script: "Defend the cause of the weak and fatherless; maintain the rights of the oppressed and poor. Rescue the weak and needy; deliver them from the hand of the wicked" (Ps. 82:3–4).

Think about the last superhero movie you saw.

What happened?

There was a problem. An evil enemy caused an imminent threat that created a need for intervention. In other words, a person, community, or planet was in grave danger and a superhero came to save the day. If they didn't, someone or everyone would die. Death is almost always the device used to draw out and employ the superhero into action. After the intervention, peace is then restored until another threat appears requiring the presence of the super savior once again.

It's the same plotline in every super-story.

Where did that idea originate?

You guessed it. God.

The Bible tells us that since the beginning of creation, an evil entity has threatened the existence of humanity.

Yes, just as every superhero story has a villain, ours does too. Unfortunately, this one is not a fictional fantasy.

His name is Satan.

Well, originally God gave him the name Lucifer along with the privilege of leading worship in God's presence. In other words, Lucifer was the angel of music, the most magnificent creature in all of God's creation at that point in time.

Lucifer was literally God's most highly decorated and dazzling angel of light, but his beauty and position of prominence eventually turned into pride. In fact, Lucifer allowed the beauty that God had given him to become the focus of his worship. Instead of leading the heavenly host of angels in worship to God, Lucifer himself wanted to be worshipped as God. This was classic idolatry, worshipping the creation instead of the Creator. So Satan led a third of the angels into rebellion against God. They waged war against God in an attempt to replace him with their leader, Lucifer.

Their efforts obviously failed and instead of overthrowing God from his heavenly throne, these demons, or hell's angels, were thrown out of heaven.

If that weren't punishment enough, Lucifer, who desired to be God, was required to live out the remainder of his days on earth in the presence of people created in the image of God.

Human beings then became a daily reminder of why Satan was removed from God's presence in the first place.

As a result, Lucifer made it his life mission to make people suffer as he was suffering. Lucifer believed that if he could make people rebel, they too would be banished from God's presence and lose their position of prominence.

Unfortunately, that is exactly what happened. The story of the Fall of Man is recorded in Genesis chapter 3.

Adam and Eve, the first people created in the image of God, were living in paradise, a form of heaven on earth known as the

Garden of Eden. The Bible tells us that God actually lived among them in the garden. They had a relationship with God and enjoyed all of God's creation. Well, almost all of it. Adam and Eve could eat from any tree in the garden except the tree of the knowledge of good and evil. That fruit was forbidden by God.

But Lucifer lied to Adam and Eve. He twisted the truth of God's word in a satanic game of semantics and led them to believe that God was not good and that being their own gods would be better. They listened to Lucifer, rebelled by eating the forbidden fruit, and lost their place of prominence in God's presence.

After that fatal bite from the forbidden fruit, death, destruction, and chaos entered God's creation. Consequently, what was once perfect was now corrupted and under the curse of sin. Everything was impacted: plants, animals, and people all sentenced to death and decay.

From that point forward, man was no longer free. Instead, all men were born into captivity, enslaved to sin, and subject to the suffering of Satan.

One would think that Satan would be satisfied after single-handedly ruining the relationship between God and his people, but he wasn't.

In fact, Satan hasn't stopped since. Every chance he gets, Satan kills, steals, and destroys. According to the Bible, that's his job description: to kill, steal, and destroy. Sounds like the job description of comic book villains isn't that original either...

Thankfully, God did not sit idly by while Satan ran rampant, wreaking havoc on humanity.

Instead, God had a plan to send a superhero, a savior, a deliverer, someone who would free the slaves, and bring justice to this evil doer, the devil.

Enter Jesus, God's Son.

His job description?

Destroy the works of the devil.

What works exactly?

We see the effects of the fall and the works of the devil in every death, addiction, sickness, war, broken relationship, famine, and fight (Acts 10:38; Luke 13:10–17). Anywhere that suffering and sin exists shows us the fingerprint of that fallen angel.

Again, Jesus's job was to fix the effects of the fall.

So after being baptized, receiving the Holy Spirit, and defying the devil's advances in the desert, Jesus is filled with dunamis power and then declares his job description to the world. While standing in a Jewish synagogue, Jesus grabbed the scroll of the prophet Isaiah and read the following:

> *The Spirit of the Lord is on me, because he has anointed me to proclaim good news to the poor. He has sent me to proclaim freedom for the prisoners and recovery of sight for the blind, to set the oppressed free, to proclaim the year of the Lord's favor. (Isa. 61:1–2)*

Jesus then sets the scroll down and states that he is the fulfillment of this prophecy, written seven hundred years prior.

The religious people are pissed.

Instead of celebrating that God's promised savior had finally arrived, the Pharisees try to kill Jesus by throwing him off a cliff. However, Jesus doesn't let that happen and splits the angry mob like Moses at the Red Sea. He then walks through the parted people and continues on with his mission. Remember, Jesus was employed by God and had a job to do!

And that is exactly what he did. From that moment forward, we see Jesus fulfilling Isaiah's prophecy by healing the sick, raising the dead, delivering people from demons, uplifting the downcast, and declaring the good news about the kingdom of God.

For three years Jesus destroyed the works of the devil and trained his disciples to do the same. For three years the disciples saw Jesus's example and heard his teaching, but they missed something.

In those three years, three times, Jesus told them that his duty, commission, and job description included the cross. Jesus told his disciples three times that he would be betrayed into the hands of the religious leaders and hung on a tree to die like a common criminal.

To the disciples, this was not good news.

Superheroes aren't supposed to die. Yet Jesus told his disciples that his greatest assignment would be completed through crucifixion.

On one occasion as Jesus predicted not only his death, but also his resurrection, the disciple Peter rebuked Jesus and said, "Never, Lord! This shall never happen to you!" Jesus responded, "Get behind me, Satan!" (Matt. 16:22–23). We see the devil's work in the doubt of the disciples, but Jesus was not distracted or deterred. Instead, knowing what was at stake, the salvation of every single person on the planet, Jesus pushed past every form of opposition to fulfill his mission.

Then, in the greatest act of love ever recorded, Jesus, the Son of God, Savior of the world, went to the cross and sacrificially laid down his life for his friends, family, and, yes, even his enemies.

This extravagant act of selfless love, and the death-defying miraculous resurrection that followed, perfectly fulfilled the plan of God and the purpose of every superhero's job description: vindicating the victims, emancipating the oppressed, pardoning the imprisoned, reversing the curse, delivering those in distress, bringing justice to the bad guy, and overall saving the day.

It was a job well done. We know that because before Jesus breathed his last and gave up the very Spirit who provided his dunamis power, Jesus said, "It is finished." Everything required to defeat the devil and save the souls of those who called on Jesus's name was completed on the cross.

His job was done, but ours was just beginning.

After Jesus resurrected from the dead, he gave his disciples their job description. He said, "Go into all the world and preach the gospel to everyone" and "make disciples of all nations, baptizing them in the name of the Father, Son, and Holy Spirit, and teaching them to obey everything I have commanded you" (Mark 16:15; Matt. 28:19–20).

As the Father employed his Son, the Son now employed his followers. And what was expected of the disciples is still our job description today. We have work to do, and God has given us the tools through our inheritance in the Holy Spirit to accomplish our assigned task.

Now that we understand the origin story, as every good superhero movie has an origin story, we will spend the rest of our time looking at how our inheritance empowers us to fulfill our God-glorifying, disciple-making, devil-destroying job description.

Be about Your Father's Business

For those wondering what it actually looks like to be employed by God, don't worry, not everyone is called to be homeless wanderers like the original disciples.

Think more superhero and less couch surfer.

Like Clark Kent, Bruce Banner, or Peter Parker, being employed by God may actually appear pretty normal. Journalists, scientists, and students, they held actual jobs. Many movie superheroes walk around their cities, contributing to society without mask, cape, or costume to separate them from those they were called to serve. It wasn't until a problem was present that the superhero employed their inherent powers.

What I'm trying to say is, don't quit your day job. You can follow Jesus full of the Holy Spirit while working as an employee, relaxing as a retired person, studying as a student, or staying home taking care of your kids. The key is to focus on your Father's business no matter your career or place of employment. Your inheritance empowers you to pursue the purposes of God by fulfilling your job description despite where you live or what you do.

An Explosive Witness

Don't forget that there is a specific purpose to our employment and empowerment, namely to glorify God by being his witnesses. Jesus said so himself: "You will receive power when the Holy Spirit comes on you; and you will be my witness…" (Acts 1:8).

If we are empowered to witness, we need to understand what that means.

When I think of witnesses, my mind goes to court.

What do witnesses do in court? They testify!

Witnesses simply express what they have seen, heard, and experienced in regard to a particular event or person. They share firsthand accounts of what happened to them or around them. A testimony is simply the telling of what you have witnessed.

Jesus wants us to testify to what God has done in our lives. We can do that with our words and the dunamis power of our inheritance.

Several years ago, I attended a pastoral refreshment weekend where we went river rafting at a Christian camp called Rock N Water. At the event, I met pastors from all across California who drove as many as seven hours to attend this retreat. That was Maurice's story anyway. Maurice was a pastor from Southern California, and somewhere between his hometown of Compton and the river, his sciatic nerve began to cause such severe pain that Maurice decided not to raft. We discovered his decision at breakfast and couldn't believe that someone would drive seven hours to sit on the sideline. That must have been some pretty powerful pain!

The circumstance was unacceptable. We wanted Maurice to raft, so our team gathered around him and began to pray, declare, and rebuke the pain away in Jesus's name. Suffice it to say, Maurice went rafting with us that day. Not only that, Maurice reported a pain-free ride. However, the moment he got off the boat, the sciatic pain returned. Although Maurice did not get to keep his healing, no one can take his testimony. All healings on this side of eternity are temporary, but the impact of our testimonies are eternal. Our testimonies even have the power to defeat the devil himself: "Then I heard a loud voice from heaven say, 'They triumphed over him by the blood of the Lamb and by the word of their testimony'" (Rev. 12:10–11).

We are empowered by the Spirit of God and provided with testimonies on purpose. Maurice now has a tangible testimony of God's healing power to accompany any presentation of the gospel message.

All throughout the gospels, Jesus testified about what God had done in the past. He also regularly reinforced his identity as the Messiah along with the message about the kingdom of God. However, many people did not believe the words of Jesus. But when Jesus healed the sick, stopped a storm, delivered someone from a demon, or another display of dunamis power, it authenticated his testimony. Many believed, not by listening to his words but through the witness of his power. Paul said it this way in reference to those who heard the gospel in the city of Thessalonica: "When we brought you the Good News, it was not only with words but also with power, for the Holy Spirit gave you full assurance that what we said was true" (1 Thess. 1:5 NLT).

Like Jesus, we are called to help people believe, not just with the bold words of the gospel and our testimonies, but also with powerful works (John 10:38).

The Holy Spirit Has Your Back

For me, as an employee of a local community college, my job description included the management and oversight of all student housing. This duty sometimes required site visits to potential housing providers, and on one particular visit, I met an elderly Indian man named Adam.

While giving me the tour of his home, I watched Adam wince and groan holding his hip with every limping step. It was obvious that Adam was in extreme pain. After seeing him ascend the many flights of steps at his hillside home in agony, I asked Adam what happened.

Adam reported that he was recently struck by a car while crossing the street. When I asked if he had received medical attention, Adam revealed that the accident happened right before I arrived and he didn't have time. Talk about commitment!

Now I knew Adam wasn't a follower of Christ. He had altars burning incense to idols all around his house, but I asked him if he knew Jesus anyway. Adam gave me the standard Hindu answer that he believes that Jesus is a god, but not the only god, as the Bible clearly teaches. He believed that all gods are essentially the same, all 350 million of them.

Instead of arguing with Adam, I testified about the healing power of Jesus. I shared that I have personally seen and experienced the miraculous healing power of Jesus in my life and provided examples. What was I doing? I was bearing witness. This was why I was empowered by the Holy Spirit, to testify!

Then, after sharing what God has done, I asked if I could pray for his back in Jesus's name and he agreed. Adam then bowed his head and placed his hands together in an eastern meditative way, and I placed my hand on his spine.

"In Jesus's name, spine align, pain leave, healing happen, according to the love of the Father and power of the Holy Spirit, in Jesus's name."

I then asked Adam if anything changed.

Adam reported that he was still in pain, so I prayed a second time.

After the second prayer, which did not differ much from the first, Adam tested out his flexibility.

First, he bent over to touch his toes. Next, Adam twisted his back from side to side. Then he started to walk, without a limp.

Adam literally walked up and down his many outside stairs without once wincing or groaning in pain.

Staring in awe at what God had just done, I heard Adam declare, "My back is healed! My back is healed!"

If that wasn't shocking enough, I then watched as Adam walked down his stairs directly to one of his tenants' doors.

After knocking, the tenant came out and Adam told the man, "You're never going to believe this, but this man is a healer sent from Jesus, and Jesus just healed my back!"

Adam was so touched by God that this Hindu man immediately started sharing his healing testimony. The excitement was obvious as the countenance on his face was completely changed and now full of joy. Adam encountered the love of God through the healing power of the Holy Spirit, and I got to participate. Best job ever!

After the incident I went home celebrating and shared the news with my wife. Later that night, I received text message after text message from Adam thanking me, praising Jesus, and asking me to come back to pray for his wife. As requested, a few days after, Alissa and I returned to pray for her.

Not only did Jesus heal her back, knees, and feet, we were also able to share the gospel, read the Bible, and pray with her.

You never know where and how the Holy Spirit will lead you. That's the adventure of following Jesus; but like a Bat-Signal in the sky, anytime we see suffering around us, this is our sign to employ the power of our inheritance.

The Principle of Persistency

Have you ever heard the saying, "If you're going to do something, do it right the first time"?

Or how about this one: "If you don't have time to do it right, when will you have time to do it over?"

Maybe it says something about the quality of my work, but I've heard that saying a lot. Mainly from my dad in regard to mowing lawns. I hated mowing lawns as a kid, but that was the only form of employment I could get in middle school.

I doubt anyone said that to Jesus, yet he once encountered a blind man who was only half healed after his first prayer attempt. Yes, I said half healed. The story can be found in Mark 8:22–26:

> They came to Bethsaida, and some people brought a blind man and begged Jesus to touch him. He took the blind man by the hand and led him outside the village. When he had spit on the man's eyes and put his hands on him, Jesus asked, "Do you see anything?"
>
> He looked up and said, "I see people; they look like trees walking around."
>
> Once more Jesus put his hands on the man's eyes. Then his eyes were opened, his sight was restored, and he saw everything clearly.

Was Jesus not powerful enough to heal this man the first time? Of course, He was powerful enough! Jesus was teaching us the principle of persistency.

The principle of persistency can be found throughout the Word of God, including the persistent widow (Luke 18), the needy neighbor (Luke 11), the fall of Jericho (Joshua 6), Naaman and the leprous king (2 Kings 5), and my favorite from Elisha the prophet in 2 Kings 13:

Right before his death, the prophet Elisha met with Jehoash, king of Israel who was fearful of going to war with the Arameans. As a prophetic word picture Elisha told the king to grab a bow and some arrows. The king was then instructed to strike the ground. King Jehoash struck the ground three times and stopped. Elisha the prophet told the king that he would only defeat the Aramean army three times, but it required five or six strikes to completely destroy them.

The principle of persistency seen in this story requires us to continue pushing until the task is completed.

What would have happened if Jesus stopped praying the first time? The blind man of Bethsaida might have continued to only see silhouettes in the shape of trees. Thank God that Jesus persisted in prayer. After the second round, the man was healed.

If the Holy Spirit employs you to pray for a person, persist until something happens. Push if you have to. I don't mean physically push them, no, Pray Until Something Happens, PUSH! Like Jesus, keep praying, keep circling, keep striking the ground, continue petitioning, and persistently pursue the breakthrough until the healing happens or the Holy Spirit provides the peace to stop.

Dealing with Disappointment

What would have happened if God had not healed Adam's back?

The answer depends on your perspective. You can either see healing as the ultimate goal and get discouraged when healing doesn't happen, or you can have a biblical perspective despite the outcome.

When describing the spiritual gifts in 1 Corinthians chapters 12–14, Paul made a point to highlight that love was the purpose of the power gifts:

> If I speak in the tongues of men or of angels, but
> do not have love, I am only a resounding gong or
> a clanging cymbal. If I have the gift of prophecy
> and can fathom all mysteries and all knowledge,
> and if I have a faith that can move mountains,
> but do not have love, I am nothing. If I give all
> I possess to the poor and give over my body to
> hardship that I may boast, but do not have love,
> I gain nothing. (1 Cor. 13:1–3)

The truth is, not every person you pray for will be healed, but they should all feel loved and they should all walk away with an understanding of the gospel, which is God's love. No matter the outcome, love is the main goal. And the love of God leads people to repentance (Rom. 2:4). That's the purpose of the power. God's love leads sinners out of their shackles and into relationship with their redeemer through repentance.

We do not inherit the power of the Holy Spirit for the sake of being superheroes. Paul said in many places that people he encountered were convinced about the love of Jesus through the power of God (Heb. 2:4; 1 Cor. 2:4, 4:20; Acts 14:3). In fact, Paul made a point to say that we cannot fully communicate the gospel without a demonstration of God's love (Rom. 15:19). Jesus even said that part of his witness were his works of power, not simply his words. The purpose of the power is to communicate the love of God through the gospel that leads people to repent.

Again, if you pray for someone and they are healed but they do not know the love of God through the gospel, what's the point? Like I said earlier, a healing miracle simple delays the inevitable. When we pursue people, the goal is for them to know God's love. Not only that, if they don't believe the gospel, they should at the very least feel loved by us. We can always carry love to the lost. That could look like a hug, an encouraging word, praying for the person's needs or tangibly meeting those needs if possible. Love is the purpose of the power.

Ultimately, we cannot control the outcome. All we are called to do is love, obey the leading of the Spirit, and share the gospel. The results rest in the hands of the Holy Spirit. This should take all the pressure off you to perform. The power is God's and so is the outcome. He alone is sovereign, and his timing can be trusted.

A Penny Saved Is a Lesson Learned

I remember when my wife and I were in debt at the start of our marriage. While golfing with a few friends from church, one of the men who I respect as a mentor mentioned that he asked God if he could pay off our loan. At this point, we still owed nearly six figures and this man wanted to pay it all off instantly.

Do you know what God said? "No, I have lessons for them to learn." God not only wanted us debt free, he never wanted us returning to those chains ever again.

What am I saying? We will never know why some prayers aren't answered. Alissa and I prayed for an angel investor to come along or a check to randomly appear on our doorstep to cover our debts, but that wasn't God's plan.

We need to understand that there are some prayers that will only be answered on the other side of eternity. It is not our job to figure out when and how God plans to answer our prayers, but it is our job to keep praying, stepping out in faith, loving people, sharing the gospel, making disciples, and releasing the dunamis power of God.

The truth is, there are some healings that will only happen in heaven. I wish it wasn't the case. I wish I had a perfect track record and every time I prayed a miracle happened, but it doesn't. For every story of a miraculous healing, I can share several that didn't happen.

During my first mission trip, my team visited a Romani village where many gypsies lived. During the day we would share the gospel on the streets; provide humanitarian aid; and invite people to our nightly church services, where many people were being saved, healed, and delivered.

While ministering in the village, we met a boy with inward-facing feet. When I say inward facing, I mean a perfect ninety-degree angle in the opposite direction. How the boy walked at all was a miracle. Well, three times on three separate occasions my team prayed for this boy and no healing miracle happened.

It was crushing.

The hope in his eyes never left, but my heart broke after every prayer void of a miraculous breakthrough. I couldn't get the boy's face out of my mind. We even returned to the same village two years later, and the boy still had inward-facing feet. Thankfully, the hope in his eyes and smile on his face never left despite his circumstances.

I had a hard time reconciling that, but God comforted me sharing that it wasn't my job to reconcile the results. My responsibility was to be obedient despite the outcome.

I've seen more than my fair share of instant and progressive miracles to know that God's power is alive and well today, but there are still healing prayers that haven't happened. Thankfully, those disappointments have been used to draw me deeper into dependency on God instead of giving up. I hope and pray the same is true for you as well.

At the end of the day, there were people in the presence of Jesus who refused to believe in him even after seeing his miracles firsthand (John 12:37). What does this tell us? We can see miracles that result in salvations, we can see miracles that do not result in salvations, and everywhere in between.

The point of the power is to love people with the gospel of God. At the very least, we plant a seed and the apostle Paul said,

> I planted the seed, Apollos watered it, but God has been making it grow. So neither the one who plants nor the one who waters is anything, but only God, who makes things grow. The one who plants and the one who waters have one purpose, and they will each be rewarded according to their own labor. For we are co-workers in God's service; you are God's field, God's building. (1 Cor. 3:6–9)

The Very Hungry Caterpillar

One of my favorite seed-sowing testimonies occurred while in my office when a Buddhist student from China came to speak with me about health insurance. After telling me about her condition, I told her about Jesus, the gospel, and the healing power of the Holy Spirit. We then prayed, nothing happened, and she left.

The student eventually came back to my office a couple months later not to report a divine healing but to inquire about which church I attended.

What happened? A seed that had been planted over a decade prior was watered during our initial conversation and prayer. The result? This woman experienced the love of Jesus and wanted more. At her request, I invited this woman to church and she hasn't stopped attending since.

In fact, within three months, she read the entire Bible. She called herself a very hungry caterpillar who couldn't get enough of the "green leaf" of the word of God. I was so intrigued and encouraged by this woman's intense pursuit of God. After asking what changed, she told me that people have been trying to convert her to Christianity for years, but it wasn't until she encountered the love of Jesus that she wanted to surrender and give God everything. From my perspective, this woman went from a Buddhist to a Bible-believing baptized Jesus follower in a few short months, but the fruit of the first planted seed actually took ten plus years to manifest.

We never know how long it will take; but your prayer, encouraging word, generous gift, gospel presentation, or act of love will accomplish God's work. Be encouraged! Your work could be the initial seed planted or the water, but God will make the seeds grow, whether we reap or sow.

Hearing for a Harvest

Speaking of sowing, I recently learned a lesson on obedience and the perspective of planting from a gift of the Holy Spirit called words of knowledge. This gift is where God tells you something about another person's life that confirms to that person that God knows them. It can be an intimate fact that no one else knows, something personal that a stranger could not possibly know, or anything else that communicates to the recipient that God sees them. It's a fun gift, but there are times when the recipient doesn't confirm or deny if the word was correct. In this case, we need to understand the concept of reaping and sowing while walking by faith and not by fruit.

Reaping is obvious; that's when we see the salvation or witness the explosive power of God's work. Sowing, on the other hand, is a secret work that is only seen once fruit comes forth. Unfortunately, the sower may not see the fruit. Sometimes they do. Many other times the seed is simply planted until someone else comes along to water that seed. Paul said either way, whether reaping or sowing, its God who makes the seed grow.

While sharing the gospel or investing your inheritance in others, your efforts may lay the groundwork by planting a seed, it may affirm the work that others have started by watering that seed, or we may reap a harvest that has been at work for quite a while. We never know which season our situation fits unless we see fruit. Neither the one who sows or waters knows which season they are in, but the one who sees the salvation or experiences the miracle does. Either way, we are called to be obedient and faithful to plant and water seeds in faith despite the fruit.

In regard to words of knowledge, I was working out at the gym when I saw a woman with a limp. While sweating on my cardio machine, I started to pray for her healing. God then told me to go talk to her, so I went.

In my conversation with this woman, I discovered that she was the victim of a DUI car accident. The seatbelt saved her life, but also slit her throat severing her spinal column. She was consequently left paralyzed. This woman was given a life sentence in a wheelchair, but God had other plans. She then told me about her progressive healing to the point where she was now walking and able to work on her fitness again.

This woman was already the recipient of a miracle, I thought maybe it wasn't for healing why I was here. I asked to pray for her anyway, and she agreed. After praying, I asked if she experienced any changes in mobility, strength, or anything else that would confirm God's work. She reported nothing. No fruit. Despite the lack of evidence, she thanked me for taking the time to talk with her and I walked away.

As I left her cardio machine and returned to mine, the Lord said, "Give her psalm 116." Not knowing what psalm 116 said, I returned to the woman and told her that God wanted her to read psalm 116 and then I left.

I had no idea what that word would accomplish, but when I got to my car, I cracked the Bible to psalm 116.

> I love the LORD, for he heard my voice;
>   he heard my cry for mercy.
> Because he turned his ear to me,
> I will call on him as long as I live.
> The cords of death entangled me,
>   the anguish of the grave came over me;
> I was overcome by distress and sorrow.
> Then I called on the name of the LORD:
>   LORD, save me!
> The LORD is gracious and righteous;
>   our God is full of compassion.
> The LORD protects the unwary;
>   when I was brought low, he saved me.
> Return to your rest, my soul,
>   for the LORD has been good to you.
> For you, LORD, have delivered me from death,
>   my eyes from tears,
>   my feet from stumbling,
> that I may walk before the LORD
>   in the land of the living.

Come on, God! Are you serious? Another translation said, "Death wrapped its roped around me." This woman had her throat cut by a type of cord or rope, almost died, wasn't able walk; and God had me share a word, "That I may walk before the Lord in the land of the living." Now, I have no idea what that word meant to that woman, but God promises that his word will never return void and will always accomplish its purpose (Isa. 55:11).

Despite the fruit, our God is faithful and our inheritance is inherently powerful. So much so that we can rest assured that when planting seeds in obedience, they will accomplish the work of God's intention. We do not need to see the fruit to remain faithful.

In fact, if all of our words fell flat, if God didn't answer another prayer, if we never experienced another miracle, God is still God and Jesus still died for our sin and still resurrected to defeat death and to give us eternal life. Our inheritance in Jesus is enough! Everything else is just a cherry on top of a perfect Resurrection sundae.

Thankfully, our God is one of abundance. Even though we don't deserve or need another miracle, he is faithful to provide, and through the inheritance of the Holy Spirit, a fruitful abundance and an awesome adventure follows.

Dentist Jesus

As a thrill seeker, one who enjoys cliff jumping, backflipping on any type of board, and tattoo collecting from foreign countries, God knew I needed a sense of adventure in my job. Thankfully, God is always faithful to provide.

One day at lunch I was brushing my teeth as a Nepalese student entered my office bathroom. We didn't make eye contact, but I recognized him from a recent interaction. After leaving the bathroom and returning to my desk, this student eventually found his way to my desk.

The student reminded me of his last visit, two months prior, when he came to request a leave of absence. This meant that the student would be returning home and not completing the semester. When I asked about the reason, he told me that he didn't have dental insurance and was in severe pain from an oral infection that was causing his gums to swell and bleed. The pain was apparently bad enough that this student was willing to lose all of his tuition and forsake his grades to fly home for dental care.

In our meeting, I told the student about Jesus and asked if I could pray for God to heal him, because, hey, what's the worst that can happen?

The student agreed, we prayed, and he left my office ready to return home to Nepal.

I didn't expect to see or hear from this student until the following semester after his dental issues were resolved; however, here he was, two months later, reporting that after our prayer, the bleeding stopped, swelling subsided, and all the pain went away. No expensive airline ticket, missed grades, painful operation, nothing. Instead, my inheritance was unleashed in the most adventurous way.

I share this testimony for God to get the glory and to reemphasize that God cannot be boxed by the Bible. There are no dental healings recorded in scripture. Yet Jesus heals teeth. There are many things that God has not recorded in his word that can still happen today. We need to be open to the adventure of the Holy Spirit, because our inheritance is anything but boring. The apostle Paul will be the first to attest...

Aikido Island

As the apostle Paul quickly discovered, being employed by Jesus was nothing short of an adventure, and a dangerous one at that. In his second letter to the church in Corinth, Paul actually recorded most of the suffering and persecution he experienced while serving the Lord. In 2 Corinthians 11:16, Paul starts off listing the countless occasions that he was beaten, flogged, and imprisoned. Then Paul described the many times that he almost died from various shipwrecks, stoning, rivers, bandits, and false believers. Paul also mentioned that five times he received the infamous thirty-nine lashes from the Jews. Each lashing was a near-death experience as it was commonly believed that forty lashes would kill the criminal.

Now, I find it interesting that out of all Paul's sufferings listed in 2 Corinthians 11, as detailed as they were, he did not mention what happened on the island of Malta in Acts chapter 27.

Before arriving at the island, Paul was once again arrested for preaching the gospel. Paul was then put in chains as a prisoner and placed on a boat headed to Rome, but the boat never arrived. Instead, a storm shipwrecked Paul, all the prisoners, and the crew of soldiers on the shores of Malta.

As the Bible records, after nearly dying at sea, then barely escaping execution by the soldiers, Paul swims to shore only to be bitten by a poisonous snake while building a fire.

This guy couldn't catch a break.

In fact, the people of Malta thought that Paul was must have been a murderer because the goddess Justice kept trying to kill him. However, an unaffected Paul shakes the snake off his hand and into a fire without suffering from the poison. The people are shocked at what they just witnessed. This man they thought was a murderer was now believed to be a god because nothing could apparently kill him.

So Paul is not only celebrated after surviving the viper bite, he was invited into the home of the highest official on the island. When he arrived at his home, Paul was introduced to the official's father who was suffering from dysentery and a fever. Paul sees the Bat-Signal, employed his Holy Spirit superpower, and healed the official's father. News spread quickly about this healing, and the whole island brought their sick to Paul, and he healed them all.

I love this!

If you watch Batman fight crime, you will notice that he utilizes a variety of fighting techniques and one of those martial arts is called aikido. This is a form of fighting and self-defense that uses the attacker's momentum as a tool. When an attacker charges Batman, he is able to use the opponent's forward motion, energy, and momentum against them. Aikido essentially enables a person to use what the enemy intended to inflict pain and suffering to instead disarm, demobilize, and detain the attacker.

Like Batman, Paul implemented the martial art of aikido and used the enemy's attack against him. Instead of allowing the viper's poisonous bite to disable or kill him, Paul used the attack as a platform to glorify God, destroy the works of the devil, and heal people. Talk about reversing the momentum!

Just as every superhero has a variety of techniques in their toolbelt, we also need to add this spiritual form of aikido to our arsenal.

This tactic is so important because the truth is, when employed by Jesus, we will get bitten!

It's just a matter of time.

Axes and Atheists

Like Paul, I was bitten on the job while building a fire.

Not by a snake, by an axe.

While chopping wood for a fire, the blade of my axe cut through a termite-infested section and bit right into my ankle.

As expected, there was blood everywhere, severe searing pain, and a panicked group of onlooking international students.

At the time of the accident, I was leading a group of students on a camping trip in Yosemite National Park. Yes, the community college actually paid me to camp. It was glorious. Not only was I now employed to enjoy my favorite family vacation spot, I got to take international students who had mostly never heard about Jesus before.

There is something about being in the woods without cell phone service that opens opportunities to talk about Jesus, and the devil hated it.

So there I was with an axe attached to my ankle. My students are screaming, I'm trying not to cry, and all I could think about was how the trip was ruined.

In need of emergency medical attention, I left my students alone in the woods without preparing dinner, providing directions, transportation, or an idea about how long I would be gone. This was a total disaster.

If that weren't dangerous enough, the hospital was two hours away and my driver was a Mongolian student without a license, driving the community college cargo van down a steep, narrow, winding mountain road. Thankfully, the pain in my ankle was distracting me from thoughts of him driving off a cliff at any moment.

After arriving safely at the hospital, the medical team cleaned the wound and gave me a handful of stitches without pain medication. Uncomfortable is an understatement.

We then turned around and drove two hours back to the campsite. It was a long five hours to be away from foreign college kids who had never camped before. Thankfully, everyone was alive when we returned, but they had obvious concerns regarding our weekend plans. I told them not to worry, that things would work out and then we all went to bed.

The next morning I woke up and could not move my leg. I was paralyzed with pain, and I had to pee, like really badly. This was not good. I lay there for a few minutes weighing out my options. There were really only two: I could pee my pants and freeze or somehow hobble my way to the bathroom. I went with the "not peeing my pants and freezing" option, and by some crazy miracle, I made it out of my tent and to my feet.

Although I was now standing, I could not put any pressure on my freshly stitched, axe-bitten ankle. As I hopped to the bathroom hoping not to lose my balance, I began to pray. That sounds too holy; it was more like complaining and arguing with God. Let's be real here.

After successfully hobbling to the bathroom and taking care of business, I headed back to camp. My prayers also continued to hobble along as my questions of "What are we supposed to do?" turned into "Lord, you have to heal me."

It was in that transition, from the questioning to the desperation, that something clicked.

I think it's called faith.

In that moment, I remembered who I was talking to. This was my Father, my Jehovah Rapha, the Lord, my Healer. I was talking to the God of Abraham, Isaac, and Jacob, the God of the Old and New Testament. I had disease-destroying, death-defeating Jesus on the phone; and my realization immediately turned my desperation into declaration.

My prayers had been so weak and powerless, but now with a proper perspective, I was able to pray, "Ankle, be healed in Jesus's name! Pain, leave right now in the name of Jesus!" The authority was real.

As I hopped and prayed, I heard, "Put your faith into practice and put some pressure on it."

I guess that makes sense. How would I know if anything happened unless it was tested?

Taking a step with my newly stitched ankle, I could feel the tenderness of the torn skin, but to my surprise, the pain began to disappear. It didn't take more than two steps to realize that the pain was completely gone. I could put the entire weight of my body on the wound, and I felt nothing. It wasn't numb, I could feel the stitches, but they didn't hurt.

I then walked back to camp without a limp. My students were confused watching me walk as though nothing traumatic had happened the night before.

They asked, "What are we going to do today?" with a tone communicating doubt that we could do what was originally planned.

"Hike North Dome," I replied.

And we did.

With a newly stitched ankle, I was able to hike eight miles, for four hours, without pain medication or any discomfort.

If that wasn't miraculous enough, on the hike I had a conversation with an atheist student from Hong Kong who asked about my faith. Earlier in the trip I tried talking to him about Jesus, but he wasn't interested. However, after witnessing the axe incident, he was all ears.

It was obvious to this atheist and the rest of the students that something miraculous had happened. I went from immobile to mountain climbing in a moment. They knew it, I knew it, and the axe incident became a platform for me to share the gospel.

However, after sharing about Jesus and answering all of the student's questions, he was still not ready to accept Jesus as his Lord and Savior. I honestly wasn't discouraged either. If anything, I was excited that the opportunity was opened to plant a seed of faith that I believed would one day bear fruit.

Thankfully, I didn't have to wait that long.

After the trip, three months later, the atheist student from Hong Kong came into my office. With a beaming smile and excitement in his eyes, he could barely contain his joy as he shared that he made the decision to follow Jesus.

(Cue fireworks)

I asked how that happened, and he admitted that there was no way he could ignore the gospel when the power of God was so clearly displayed through the axe incident.

I was ecstatic!

There is nothing more exciting than when someone accepts Jesus in faith and goes from death to life.

Yes, God healed my ankle and that was a miracle, but nothing compares to raising the dead. Jesus agreed. He told his disciples that there is a party in heaven when even one sinner repents (Luke 15:10). We partied that day, celebrating what God had done: bringing a man from death to life.

Friends, that is spiritual aikido and dunamis power in action. Jesus took what the devil intended for evil and flipped it for his glory. Through our inheritance, God has equipped us to fight the devil and set captives free. This is our job description.

Snakebites and Firefights

If you haven't already figure this out, working for Jesus is not for the faint at heart.

On one of my mission trips to Romania, I remember being asked to visit the house of a demon-possessed boy. Having watched many horror movies about demonic possession, my imagination was racing about what might happen. I was thinking about spinning heads, green projectile puke, all the good Hollywood stuff; but none of that happened.

Instead, when we arrived, my team was greeted by the boy's deeply distressed and grieving parents. They introduced us to their son, who looked completely normal. On the surface, there was no indication that anything demonic was going on, but the second we mentioned the name of Jesus, everything changed. The boy began to scream, wail, and moan with deep, dark demonic noises. His eyes rolled to the back of his head with only the bloodshot whites showing while his face began to twist and contort. Then came the superhuman strength. This boy could not have been more than ten years old or weigh more than eighty pounds, but he had the strength of five grown men. It literally took five adults to hold this kid on the couch as we commanded the demons to leave. I remember the boy grabbing my hand as we prayed and feeling my bones being crushed by his grip. It hurt!

He continued to thrash around as we declared the authority of Jesus, but the fight didn't last long. It never does. The demons left, the boy became quiet, his face returned to normal, and there was a peaceful stillness that replaced the once demonic storm.

This was one of my first tangible experiences with spiritual warfare. The Romanian boy was in bondage to the devil, but the power of the Holy Spirit set that captive free.

Our team celebrated like when Jesus sent out his seventy-two disciples to implement their inheritance and returned with many praise reports, saying, "Lord, even the demons submit to us in your name" (Luke 10:17).

I expected Jesus to celebrate their victory over demons. Instead, Jesus said, *"I saw Satan fall like lightning from heaven. I have given you authority to trample on snakes and scorpions and to overcome all the power of the enemy; nothing will harm you. However, do not rejoice that the spirits submit to you, but rejoice that your names are written in heaven" (Luke 10:18–20).* Then again in Mark 16, Jesus said, *"And these signs will accompany those who believe: In my name they will drive out demons; they will speak in new tongues; they will pick up snakes with their hands; and when they drink deadly poison, it will not hurt them at all; they will place their hands on sick people, and they will get well."*

According to these two passages, Jesus promised us that we have authority over demons and that these spiritual snakes and scorpions will not harm us. In fact, Jesus says, nothing, literally "no" "thing" will harm us.

However, Paul got bit by a snake and I'm sure that hurt! My hand got crushed, and I took an axe in the ankle.

How do we reconcile that?

Jesus explicitly said to celebrate that our names are written in heaven, not that we won't get hurt or that demons submit to us. The focus of this phrase was the fact that followers of Jesus are saved. We are saved from the inevitable damnation coming to all demonic forces of darkness.

Snakes can bite us, bad things can happen, but they cannot steal our salvation. Like I said earlier, if you aggravate a viper long enough, you are bound to get bit, but no one and nothing can harm our inheritance.

This may be news to some, but the second you joined Team Jesus, a huge bull's-eye was placed on your back. You better believe that Satan has his sights on you.

Friends, you need to hear this:

There is a war going on for your soul! Satan hates you. The devil is real, and he wants to destroy you. So do not be surprised when trouble comes. Jesus warned us that it would (John 16:33). Trials, temptations, attacks—all of these things have been promised, but in the same breath Jesus said, "Take heart!" Why? Because Jesus has overcome the world! He defeated death. He destroyed the works of the devil and has empowered us to do the same.

However, in the face of fear, it can be easy to forget this truth so God repeated over and over again, over 365 times in his Word, "Do not fear!"

We do not need to fear spiritual warfare. Instead, take heart! In reference to Satan and his legion of losers, God's word in 1 John 4:4 encourages us that "the one in you (the Holy Spirit) is greater than the one in the world (Satan)."

A Ray of Light

A Chinese student named Ray came into my office for visa advice and counseling, a common occurrence at my place of employment. He reported the inability to sleep, focus on school, or think

138

clearly. Ray was also hearing voices, seeing dark figures in his bedroom, and suffered from debilitating fear and anxiety.

After sharing the gospel with Ray, I prayed for him asking the Holy Spirit to deliver him from the spirit of fear, anxiety, and rebuking all other demonic oppression in his life. Ray left my office in tears, thanking God and reported back to my office weeks later that he was sleeping, thinking clearly, no longer hearing voices, or seeing demons in his room. Ray immediately started attending and leading in the International Student Christian club on campus.

In 1 Corinthians 4:20, Paul said, *"The kingdom of God is not a matter of talk, but of power."* Our inheritance has the explosive dunamis power to set captives free. It doesn't matter what work of the devil has enslaved an individual: fear, addiction, the occult, unforgiveness...you name it, the Holy Spirit can destroy it. There is power in the name of Jesus!

The presence of darkness cannot compete with the light. The second that the power of the light shows up, darkness is driven away. Just ask the light switch. When you flip it, what happens? Darkness flees! It's the same in spiritual warfare. A single ray of God's light is always the majority. Satan doesn't stand a chance in the presence of the Holy Spirit.

I ask again, will we experience physical harm as we follow Jesus? Absolutely. No superhero fights unscathed. Even if we lose our lives in battle—and many believers do, just ask the disciples—no satanic spirit can steal our salvation. It doesn't matter if we are crucified upside down like Peter; beheaded like Paul; burned, stoned, boiled or speared to death like the rest of the disciples, we are still victorious in Christ over the spiritual death that awaits Satan and his demons.

So when Satan strikes—notice I said "when" and not "if"— when Satan strikes, we need to ask the question, how can God take what the enemy intended for evil and turn it for God's glory and the good of others? How can the snake bites in your life result in the healing of others? How can the mess communicate the message of the gospel?

Remember, Paul was bitten by a poisonous snake, denied death its victory, threw the snake into the fire, and used that platform to bring healing to the people of Malta. This sounds a lot like Jesus. In the same way, our story too, with all the scrapes, bites, and bruises, can communicate the gospel and bring healing to many through our inheritance in the Holy Spirit.

Silence the Snake

Now remember, we are still talking about our job description as superheroes empowered by the Holy Spirit. As every superhero has an archnemesis, so does the Spirit-filled Christ follower. And you had better believe that your particular place of employment, aka the kingdom of God, has competition. So follow me as we continuing to discover who this devil is and how to overcome his opposition.

Satan, our adversary, takes many forms and has a multitude of names. He is known as the father of lies, the accuser, and the deceiver just to name a few. In the Garden of Eden, we understand how he got some of those names as he deceives Eve into believing a lie about God's word. But what was the lie? To understand how our enemy operates, we need to look back in time to see his tactics in detail.

In Genesis 2:16, after God brought Adam to life, he was given a God guided tour of the garden, which was his home and inheritance. After viewing everything that was created for his enjoyment and employment, God specifically told Adam, "You are free to eat from any tree in the garden; but you must not eat from the tree of the knowledge of good and evil, for when you eat from it, you will certainly die."

One chapter later, in Genesis 3, Satan enters the scene and starts a conversation with Adam and Eve. He slithered, "Did God really say, 'You must not eat from any tree in the garden'?"

We see his tactics from the very start of the conversation. Satan wanted Adam and Eve to doubt the word of God by asking, "Did God really say?"

He does the same thing today.

Did God really say that marriage is only between a man and a woman?

Did God really say there are only two genders?

Did God really say all sexual activity outside of the marriage covenant is sin?

Did God really say that life starts at conception and abortion is murder?

Did God really say to keep the marriage bed pure?

Did God really say that homosexuality is sin?

Did God really say that drunkenness is a sin and to maintain a sober mind?

Did God really call sin, sin and require people to repent?

Did God really say?

Yes. Yes, he did.

Eve responds to the snake's question, "We may eat fruit from the trees in the garden, but God did say, 'You must not eat fruit from the tree that is in the middle of the garden, and you must not touch it or you will die'" (Gen. 3:2–3).

This was the correct response, but watch what Satan says next: "You will not certainly die, for God knows that when you eat from it your eyes will be opened, and you will be like God, knowing good and evil" (Gen. 3:4–5).

Watch the progression.

Satan started by planting a seed of doubt by questioning the word of God. He then twisted the word of God and injected a lie, "You will not certainly die." But what happened next is the worst deception of all.

"When you eat it, you will be like God."

Since the beginning of the garden, Satan's tactic has remained the same. Satan tempts people to sin in order to receive what God has already given them.

God already made Adam, Eve, and all of humanity in his likeness and image. They were already like God. But Satan suggested that eating the forbidden fruit and rebelling against God is what would actually make them like God.

He did the same thing to Jesus.

In the desert, when Jesus was fasting for forty days, Satan tempted Jesus with all the kingdoms of the world at the cost of Jesus's worship. Again, Satan with the worship thing.

He said, "All of this I will give to you if you bow down and worship me" (Matt. 4:9).

How stupid is this snake? Jesus created everything! He could have any earthly kingdom he wanted, but his only concern was the kingdom of heaven and that came only with obedience to his Father.

Once again, Satan was tempting someone to sin in order to receive what already belonged to them.

If Satan had the audacity to try this tactic with Jesus, the Son of God, surely, he will try it with us.

And he does!

The number one thing that Satan tempts us with is something called righteousness.

Simply put, righteousness is right standing with God, and Satan tries to get us to believe that we are not in right standing with our Heavenly Father.

Since righteousness is something that Jesus purchased for us on the cross, Satan tempts us to sin by working for what is already ours. Why would that be a sin? It's the rebellion of unbelief. God's word tells us that we are righteous, but Satan's word tells us that we need to work for it (2 Cor. 5:21; 1 Cor. 1:30; Rom. 3:21–22, 4:5).

Anytime I fail, fall, or stumble in sin, Satan is right there to remind me that I blew it. He tells me that I'm not righteous. He tells me that I'm not worthy. He tells me that the only way for me to reenter God's presence is to pay with my own religious works. He tempts me to do good deeds to pay my own sin debt. He wants me to sin to receive the righteousness that Jesus already bought for me with his blood.

Satan essentially temps us with self-righteousness. The belief that our works can make us right with God. Self-righteousness is doing the right things with the wrong motives. These are called dead works, which could be good things like reading the Bible, serving in church, praying, praising, fasting and giving. These are all right things, but not if you're doing them to attain righteousness. Doing good deeds to receive righteousness is the definition of dead works.

And again, that is the snake's strategy. He tempts us to earn through dead works what God has already given us by grace.

You have an inheritance from God! His provision, protection, purpose, peace, power, and presence are yours. As a child of God, you belong to God and God belongs to you. Your Father has given you an inheritance in the Holy Spirit. Through Jesus, you have every spiritual blessing in heaven (Eph. 1:3). You don't need to sin, rebel, or work dead deeds to receive it.

The next time Satan comes slithering along to tempt you, like Jesus, silence that snake with the word of God! Remind him that you are righteous! Remind him of God's promise that "there is now no condemnation for those in Christ Jesus" (Rom. 8:1). Wield the word of God like a sword and silence that snake!

Did you know the Bible is described as being sharper than any double-edged sword (Heb. 4:12)? Yes, and that's not the only piece of armor and weaponry God has provided. We'll jump into all the armor of God in the next section, but the word of God cuts through the lies of the devil like light piercing through darkness. We need to know the word of God. If we don't know the truth, how can we discern lies?

That's not meant to be an indictment, but an invitation. If you don't know the word of God and you feel vulnerable to the enemy's attacks, it's time to arm yourself. Prepare for battle by reading, reciting, reflecting, memorizing, and writing the word of God on your heart. What are you waiting for? Pick up the sword and start swinging.

Protective Power

Are you aware that every superhero has armor?

It doesn't matter how inherently powerful and well equipped, every superhero has protective gear. They may have massive muscles like the Hulk or a steel suit like Superman, but every superhero has armor.

And so do we, which begs the question...

Why would God give us armor for our employment unless we actually had an enemy and a need?

You see, sin not only separates us from God and grieves the Holy Spirit, it diminishes our ability to resist the devil who is described as a roaring lion looking for someone to devour. If there is a roaring lion looking at you for his next meal, you had better be ready to run or resist, stand, and fight. Thankfully, in Paul's last paragraphs to the church in Ephesus, he showed us how:

> *Finally, be strong in the Lord and in his mighty power. Put on the full armor of God, so that you can take your stand against the devil's schemes. For our struggle is not against flesh and blood, but against the rulers, against the authorities, against the powers of this dark world and against the spiritual forces of evil in the heavenly realms. Therefore, put on the full armor of God, so that when the day of evil comes, you may be able to stand your ground, and after you have done everything, to stand. Stand firm then, with the belt of truth buckled around your waist, with the breastplate of righteousness in place, and with your feet fitted with the readiness that comes from the gospel of peace. In addition to all this, take up the shield of faith, with which you can extinguish all the flaming arrows of the evil one. Take the helmet of salvation and the sword of the Spirit, which is the word of God. (Eph. 6:10–17)*

These verses always get me hyped. We are called to be warriors! It's evident in the demon-defying, devil-destroying wardrobe that God has given us: helmets, swords, shields—all ready for war.

We have been called to fight a spiritual battle against our spiritual adversary.

Did you notice that we are not called to fight against people?

People are not the opposition. We never win when we fight our neighbors. People are not the problem.

It's the satanic power of sin, demonic oppression, and devilish influence that causes people to attack other people. This is the reason that God has sent us on a rescue mission to save people with the message of the gospel and the power of the Holy Spirit.

Since we are fighting a spiritual battle against Satan and his demons, we have been equipped with spiritual armor. We need the full armor of God! Let me say that differently. We need to constantly remind ourselves of our righteousness, salvation, the peace we have with God; the presence of God with us through his word and Spirit; the truth of the message we carry; and the faith God has given us to complete our commission.

You better believe that Satan will attack us in every one of these areas, especially when we fall. There's that *when* word again. We will fall. We will get knocked down. We are still susceptible to sin, but sin no longer has the power to control us. As Christ followers, as reborn and adopted children of God, we are controlled by the spirit of God, not our sinful fleshly desires. But since sin still happens, God was very strategic about this armor, knowing exactly how the enemy would attack.

The Conundrum of Condemnation

When God equipped us for our employment with his armor, He was well aware of our archnemesis. God knew his name. In Hebrew, the name *Satan* actually means "the accuser." God wanted to protect us against Satan's accusations. The Old Testament accounts in Job and Zechariah are great examples of Satan's accusatory attacks, but we don't see this happening in the New Testament. Why?

The devil knows the truth. Satan understands that the blood of Jesus is sufficient to cover all of our sins, so he doesn't accuse us to God. We don't see a single example of this in the New Testament. Satan knows that Jesus resurrected and defeated death, so accusing us to God is a losing battle. Instead, his accusations are meant to convince us that we stand condemned in God's heavenly courts. Satan uses condemnation to accomplish the goal of his accusations.

According to *Webster*, *condemnation* is the sentencing of someone to a particular judgment, especially death.

The result?

Condemnation keeps us from pursuing God's presence due to the fear of judgment.

If Satan can persuade us of this lie, we won't pursue God and we surely won't pursue the prisoners that the devil keeps in captivity. His accusations are meant to disarm, discourage, and dissuade us from fulfilling our devil-destroying job description.

Condemnation is so powerful it can even render our inheritance as powerless! Now, condemnation cannot actually take the power from our inheritance, but it can persuade us to believe a lie by distorting our perception. From experience, it is really hard to share the good news and show God's love when we believe the lie that God has condemned us.

The good news is, a lie is only powerful if we believe it, just as the truth only empowers us if we embrace it. It's true! We only believe what we actually do. In other words, believing is doing. Jesus said it this way, in reference to our inheritance of miracles, signs, and wonders: "These signs will follow those who believe" (Mark 16:17–19). We do what we believe, whether we believe the truth or a lie.

So if the snake's strategy is to tempt us with righteousness through dead works, what is God's strategy to stop the snake?

In the book of Numbers, there is a story in the twenty-first chapter about snakes that describes his plan prophetically in detail.

Israel had just escaped slavery in Egypt and is now being led through the desert by Moses, with God as their personal provider and protector.

As the people progress toward the Promised Land, they start to grumble and complain against God. Specifically, about the choice of food. The people are not satisfied with the manna from heaven that God has been providing, so he sends snakes to attack the people. The people are bitten, many die, and the rest cry out to Moses to stop the snake attack.

Let's pick up the story in Numbers 21:8–9:

> *So Moses prayed for the people. The LORD said to Moses, "Make a snake and put it up on a pole; anyone who is bitten can look at it and live." So Moses*

made a bronze snake and put it up on a pole. Then when anyone was bitten by a snake and looked at the bronze snake, they lived.

What does this story have to do with righteousness? Everything. Check this out.

Everything involved to execute the judgment of sin through the Old Testament sacrificial system occurred on a bronze altar with bronze tools. Again, everything used to slaughter the animal sacrifices for sin were bronze. Why? Because bronze in the Bible represents judgment.

Going back to the Garden of Eden, after the snake tempts Adam and Eve into sin, God curses the snake. The snake then became a representation of sin's curse.

Combining the two, we see the bronze snake on a pole as a picture of God's judgment against the curse of sin. Sound anything like Jesus on the cross?

If not, let me elaborate.

In the book of Deuteronomy 21:23, God says, "Cursed is anyone hung on a tree." Both the snake and people hung on trees were cursed. Jesus was hung on a wooden cross. And we know that wood comes from trees. Since Jesus was hung on a wooden cross, he became the curse of sin (Gal. 3:13).

Going back to our story in the desert, anyone bitten by the cursed snakes that looked to the bronze snake was healed. This was a picture of what God planned to do for his people who were bitten by the curse of sin.

Now, because Jesus became sin, although he himself was sinless, and allowed God to completely punish and condemn that sin on the cross, when we look at the finished work of Jesus, we too are healed, forgiven, freed from condemnation, and made righteous.

Both actions required a step of faith. To look at a bronze snake instead of seeing a doctor was a step of faith for the Israelites. For us, looking to the finished work of Jesus, instead of working religiously doing dead works to earn right standing with God, is an act of faith. And Hebrews 11:6 says, "Without faith, it is impossible to please God."

Double Jeopardy

We need to stop here. This is so important!

When people make a costly mistake on the jobsite, many immediately fear discipline, punishment, or fines from the manager. The same is true when people hear about the story of the snakes, or the great flood, or the destruction of Sodom and Gomorrah, or any other story from the Old Testament telling of God's anger, judgment, and wrath, people start to wonder what will happen to them when they sin. They want to know when snakes will come out to bite them.

People see a God quick to punish sin in the Old Testament and assume that God will respond in the same way now.

However, three simple words forever changed the course of history. At the end of the crucifixion, after Jesus was brutally beaten, tortured, and nailed to the cross. After all of God's anger, wrath, and judgment fell on his Son, Jesus said, "It is finished".

What was finished?

The requirements of righteousness, dead works, Old Testament law, the payment and punishment for sin, the curse—all of it was now finished. There's now nothing more to add, Jesus paid it all.

Earlier I mentioned that sin makes us hide from God, like Adam and Eve in the garden. However, 1 John 4:18 says, "There is no fear in love. But perfect love drives out fear, because fear has to do with punishment."

When we feel that we can't enter God's presence in fear of punishment, we need to be reminded of a legal term called *double jeopardy*.

In a court of law, when someone is charged, found guilty, and punished for a crime, they can never be punished for the same crime again.

Double jeopardy is still in play today. You did the crime; Jesus paid the penalty. The fullness of God's wrath was already executed on his Son for every crime we have ever committed against God. It is finished.

Can I dig into this a little bit?

According to Hebrews 1:3 Jesus finished his work on the cross and then sat down at the right hand of the Father. Then, Ephesians 2:6 says that, "We too are seated with Christ in the heavens."

Before any of this happened, a crowd of people asked Jesus what works God required of them to be acceptable to God. Jesus could have given a laundry list of religious deeds that needed to be done, but listen to what he said. In John 6:29, Jesus responded, "Your work is to believe in the one God sent."

Did you catch that?

Our work is to believe in the one who has made us righteous. In other words, our job is to rest in our righteousness. The religious work was finished so we could receive right standing with God because of his work, not ours.

This does not mean that we now have a license to live a fruitless, idle life.

How many of you have heard the phrase, "Choose a job you love, and you'll never work a day in your life?"

The same is true for the righteous saints who have placed their faith in the finished work of Jesus. We will partner with God to pursue people and his purposes, but these are no longer dead works. We are now free to live, love, and serve from a place of security in our right standing with God.

Put the dead works to death. By faith, we are free!

This is not just a free ticket to heaven. Jesus came to set us free from condemnation here and now. He wants us to live abundantly free. We all know too many Christians today who are saved but still living in bondage.

So how do we walk in freedom?

Dump the debt, embrace accusations, apply repellent, and silence the snake! Follow me through the next few sections, and I'll show you how.

Dump the Debt

Earlier, I told the story of how my wife and I spent nearly three years getting out of undergraduate debt. Every single month for almost three years we sent checks to the bank until we received the notice that said our debt was paid in full.

How ridiculous would it be for us to have ignored that letter and continued writing checks every month?

This is what we do with God when we listen to the lies of Satan and work for our righteousness.

God is telling us that our debt has been paid in full, and yet we continue writing religious checks. Checks that essentially say, "Sorry, God, I don't believe that sacrificing your Son was enough to cover my sin, so here's another payment."

That wouldn't be just foolish, it would be downright offensive.

Dump the debt; it's been paid in full.

Embrace the Accusations

We also need to understand that there is usually some truth to what the snake is saying. That's why he is called the deceiver. He twists the truth to lead us astray.

So when you hear the snake's accusations, embrace the truth.

Acknowledge the accuracy of his accusations while also acknowledging the reality of your righteousness.

The accusations are true and deserving of death, but Jesus died in your place, so there is now no condemnation and no double jeopardy.

Romans 5:16 says, "Adam's sin led to condemnation, but God's free gift leads to our being made right with God even though we are guilty of many sins." According to this scripture, the truth is that we are guilty, but God's gift made us righteous.

So every time the snake reminds you of sin, remind him of God's Son. Every time you are accused, remind the snake about Christ, who broke the curse on the cross by taking the torture himself.

Apply Repellent

Before we talk about snake repellent, I want to issue a warning:

Our righteousness does not give us the right to continue in sin. Let me say that again. God's grace is not a license to sin. First Corinthians 15:34 says, "Awake to righteousness and sin no more."

Now that we've read the warning label on the snake repellent, let's check out the directions.

It reads, "To apply, repent."

When the woman from John chapter 8 was caught in adultery by the religious leaders, Jesus silenced their accusations and then told the woman, "I don't condemn you, but leave your life of sin." Jesus was inviting this woman to repent, to leave her life of sin, and to change her ways. This is repentance, and it repels the snake.

Repentance repels the snake by turning us away from lies and turning us back toward the truth. Repentance reminds us of the truth that we are saved, we are righteous, we have peace with God, we have an inheritance, that God's word and promises are true, that the Spirit of God is with us; and this truth repels the snake and revives our faith.

There is power in repentance and again, there is "There is now NO CONDEMNATION for those in Christ Jesus" (Rom. 8:1).

No snake can stop you with the knowledge that God accepts and supports you. Literally, "If God is for us, who can be against us?" (Rom. 8:31). So never get out of bed without first putting on the full armor of God. Then, once fully clothed in the confidence of God's unfailing love and acceptance, the flaming arrows from the father of lies will fall flat at our feet.

Friends, we have a job to do! Put on your armor and let's get to work.

Know Your Kryptonite

Clark Kent may be faster than a speeding bullet, more powerful than a locomotive, able to leap tall buildings in a single bound, and bend steel with his bare hands; but Superman is also well-known for his weakness. It doesn't matter how powerful of an inheritance Superman received from his parents; kryptonite could still cripple him.

This word *kryptonite* is synonymous for anything that can seriously weaken or harm an individual.

Do you know your kryptonite?

Satan does.

Lucifer has been around long enough to know all the weaknesses of humanity. King Solomon told us that nothing is new under the sun, including the condition of the human heart. Our enemy and adversary, the devil, knows this and has become an expert at exposing and exploiting our weaknesses. Which is why we need to be armed with truth, especially in the areas of our weakness.

Would you allow a burglar to break into your home through the same window every night? No! Once you understood his strategy, you would reinforce that window with steel bars. The strategy should be no different with Satan. Wherever the enemy is able to access you and your inheritance, build boundaries and set up security. Whether you struggle with pornography, sexual purity, loneliness, substance abuse, anger, apathy, laziness, or lust, look for verses in the Bible to combat those kryptonian attacks.

Although no one can take our inheritance in the Holy Spirit, you can be rendered powerless and ineffective if you allow the father of lies to lead you into sin.

Paul wrote a letter to his spiritual son Timothy, telling him that his inheritance would be most impactful if he kept himself pure and protected from sin. We read Paul's words here in 2 Timothy 2:19–22:

> Everyone who confesses the name of the Lord must turn away from wickedness. In a large house there are articles not only of gold and silver, but also of wood and clay; some are for special purposes and some for common use. Those who cleanse themselves from the latter will be instruments for special purposes, made holy, useful to the Master and prepared to do any good

work. Flee the evil desires of youth and pursue righteousness, faith, love and peace, along with those who call on the Lord out of a pure heart.

Remember, the devil has a job description: "to kill, steal, and destroy." If he can get you to believe his lies and lead you into sin, you can be spiritually crippled like Clark Kent. Again, if Satan can convince you to rebel to receive what God has already given you, he can steal your strength.

Satan doesn't even need you to overtly sin for him to win. Another form of covert or undercover kryptonite is complacency.

Again, the devil is well aware of what you carry. He knows you have the dunamis power to destroy what he has done and is currently doing. The devil knows that the message of the gospel can set captives free and break any chain of oppression. He knows that if he can convince you to become complacent, you won't care about the call on your life.

This is why Paul prayed,

> For this reason, since the day we heard about you, we have not stopped praying for you. We continually ask God to fill you with the knowledge of his will through all the wisdom and understanding that the Spirit gives, so that you may live a life worthy of the Lord and please him in every way: bearing fruit in every good work, growing in the knowledge of God, being strengthened with all power according to his glorious might so that you may have great endurance and patience, and giving joyful thanks to the Father, who has qualified you to share in the inheritance of his holy people in the kingdom of light. (Col. 1:9–11)

We have been exhorted and encouraged not to forget our call and to make sure we walk in a manner worthy of the Lord Jesus. Which is why we must combat the devil to fight against the kryptonian effects of complacency. Things like television, social media, video games, hobbies, even an excessive amount of Bible study groups and religious church activities can lull people into complacency.

Let's be honest, how many Bible studies do we need to attend before actually putting the power of God into practice? We are in a war here, people! The devil knows that if he can keep us complacent, whether that's on the couch or within the four walls of the church, we cannot be effective in fighting the spiritual battle for souls.

When it comes down to it, complacency is just as sinful as anything else that dishonors God. James 4:17 makes this quite clear: "Whoever knows the right thing to do and fails to do it, for him that is sin."

Thankfully, the antidote is always accessible. Repentance is within arm's reach. God's word says, "If we confess our sins, he is faithful and just and will forgive our sins and purify us of all unrighteousness" (1 John 1:9). At any moment we can call on the name of Jesus, repent of our sin, and our Savior will swoop in like Superman and deliver us from the devil. Not only that, as we submit ourselves to God, we are able to resist Satan and our strength returns (James 4:7).

Losing Our Life Group

Why have I been talking so much about Satan? Because destroying the devil's work is part of our job description. However, fulfilling that duty is impossible if we don't truly believe that he exists. One of Satan's greatest tactics is to convince people that his existence is fiction, not fact. His goal is to blind people to the demonic spiritual reality all around them, so we blame one another instead of engaging the enemy who is behind every act of sin in humanity.

My wife and I once led a Bible study for high school students. I personally started with this particular group during their freshmen year and spent every Wednesday for four years watching these students grow their relationship with the Lord. As we read through the Bible together, specific topics would come up but we noticed that we never talked about spiritual warfare.

Well, part of our role as shepherds is to protect the sheep, and we were aware of many students experiencing spiritual attacks. The problem was that they had no idea what was actually happening. They thought tormenting dreams, dark shadowy figures in their bedrooms at night, addiction, intrusively abusive thoughts, and suicidal ideations were a normal part of life.

To an extent, they were right but not for the reasons they believed. Many of our students watched horror movies and thought that these happenings were connected to what they were watching. In a sense, they were but many believed it was simply their imaginations running wild.

We knew the truth and wanted to set them free.

So we started a Bible study on spiritual warfare. The first night we watched a movie about a group of Christians following the Holy Spirit to the darkest places in society to shine the light and love of Jesus. These Christians went to New Age festivals, witchcraft conventions, and other cultic places where demonic practices were the norm. In each scene, these Christ followers would share the gospel, pray for the demonized, and watch their dunamis power set people free from demonic oppression. It was incredible.

However, one student abruptly left our home in the middle of the movie. We didn't think much of it at the time, but we soon discovered that the student thought we were deceived to believe this stuff was real. The parents sadly agreed. None of them thought that spiritual warfare was an appropriate topic for kids. More than that, they believed we were heretics for teaching that Satan and demons were real. The worst part was that without entertaining a conversation or addressing their concerns with us, the parents of this student convinced the other parents to keep their kids out of our home.

Through willful ignorance, Satan was able to kill, steal, and destroy something that was spiritually enriching, equipping, and empowering for these students.

Thankfully, God eventually restored our relationship with that student and others in the group many years later. However, the reality remains that Satan wants to distract and deceive people about his presence and participation in their lives.

Expensive Inheritance

As with many heroic lines of duty, our job description comes with a cost. Following Jesus could cost you a life group like us or maybe a career, an accumulated fortune, family member, or even more. We follow in the footsteps of a man who loved his friends, family, and enemies to death; why would our lives look any different?

That question was rhetorical, but it implies the importance of counting the cost. Jesus had a lot to say about this, but it's simply logical. If I considered a career as a police officer, fire fighter, or a position in the armed forces, I would need to account for the possibility of making the ultimate sacrifice. The same is true when making the decision to follow Jesus, who laid down his life to save ours, and he has called us to do the same for others.

The truth is, there are millions of Christian martyrs in our history and many of those deaths happen today, during our lifetime. The bottom-line, sharing the gospel can cost your very life. There are places all around the globe where Christians are murdered every day for sharing about the Messiah. Yes, you can get killed for sharing about Christ, but most people will only experience a much lesser form of persecution such as ridicule and rejection. Either way, love requires a sacrifice, a willingness to say, "Christ died to save my soul, and I will share his love with the lost, no matter the cost." That's what it means to carry our cross.

Christians are those who have counted the cost and committed themselves to the teachings of Jesus who actually commanded his followers to carry their own cross. Does this mean a literal death? Not necessarily. But to some, absolutely. It is human nature to avoid discomfort at any cost, but the call of Jesus is to embrace discomfort by bringing the message of the gospel to people who are perishing.

Carrying our cross means listening to the words of the Lord Jesus, who said, "There is no greater love than to lay down your life for your friends" (John 15:13). Carrying our cross is an acknowledgment that persecution may come, but that we will go anyway.

Love was never meant to be free. It cost Jesus everything. Our inheritance was expensive. Our salvation and the inheritance of the

Holy Spirit literally cost the lifeblood of the only begotten Son of God.

We received an expensive inheritance. One that was extremely costly to purchase and often equally as costly to provide to others, yet this is our call—a call that comes with great reward.

Invested Inheritance

During the final phase of the Peter Parker Process, the best and most blessed part of our employment are the dividends of discipleship.

Did you know that discipleship pays dividends?

It does!

We are all part of the body of Christ from the oldest disciple to the newest convert. And as we have discovered together, every believer is inhabited by the Holy Spirit. The Holy Spirit is our inheritance who also gives us gifts. Those gifts are purposed, as Paul said in Ephesians 4:12 to "equip his people for works of service, so that the body of Christ may be built up until we all reach unity in the faith and in the knowledge of the Son of God and become mature, attaining to the whole measure of the fullness of Christ."

What does this mean?

When we fulfill our job description by destroying the works of the devil and making disciples, we are adding more people with more power and more gifts to our family. Those disciples are then equipped and empowered to serve. Remember, the gifts are for service, not status. The gifts are meant to be a sign pointing lost people to the Messiah and a tool to build the body of Christ.

As disciples are made, apostles, prophets, evangelists, pastors, and teachers are added to our community, aka the kingdom of God. Those disciples are gifted with the ability to heal, prophesy, work miracles, help, guide, generously give, share words of knowledge, discern spirits, speak in and interpret tongues, and do all the same things that Jesus did. Disciples equipped with dunamis-empowered gifts are then released into the world to use their inheritance to bless and build the body of Christ, aka you and me. These are the dividends of discipleship.

This may be news to some, but everyone needs ministry. No one is exempt. We all need to be encouraged. We all need healing, deliverance, hope, guidance, affirmation, confirmation, revelation, understanding, counseling, and all the ministry benefits of the Holy Spirit working through his people. As disciple makers, we give but we also receive the same in the form of ministry and the fruit of the spirit.

Yes, another dividend of discipleship is fruit. As we follow Jesus, walking step by step with the Holy Spirit, we become like the one leading us. We always do. Our lives always reflect whoever is leading us. Be careful who you follow. But we can be certain, expectant, and excited about following Jesus because the Holy Spirit is conforming us to his likeness and restoring the image of God in us that was tainted by sin.

Yes, as we follow Jesus, we begin to look and act like Jesus. In fact, through this sanctification process, our lives will produce the fruit of love, joy, peace, patience, kindness, goodness, gentleness, faithfulness, and self-control (Gal. 5:22). This will be the natural or supernatural overflow.

And who does fruit benefit? Yes, the tree, but others as well, you and me! The people around the tree benefit from the fruit. That means, another dividend of discipleship is fruit from your life and fruit from the lives of others for you to enjoy. The end goal? We enjoy all the fruit of the Garden of Eden as God intended. These are just a few of the dividends of discipleship.

I've said it now several times, but it is worth repeating: Jesus was very clear that our job description included making disciples. He said, "Make disciples of all nations, baptizing them in the name of the Father, Son, and Spirit and teaching them to obey everything I have commanded" (Matt. 28:19). Our inheritance was meant to be invested, to grow, and to pay dividends.

A Righteous Retirement

Before we continue any further on the topic of rewards, it's important to understand that the Good News and the Great

Commission do not contradict one another. In fact, they are complimentary. Like Batman and Robin, Superman and Wonder Woman, or the Avengers, the Good News and the Great Commission go hand in hand.

The Good News, otherwise known as the Gospel, is all about what God has done for us, not what we have or have not done for him. Our faith in the finished work of Jesus is what saves us.

Notice that Jesus did not make the Great Commission a requirement to receive salvation. The Great Commission, the chance to partner with God, is a privilege not a prerequisite.

The work of making disciples, our employment, does not determine our righteousness. No. It's dead religion that requires work to receive righteousness, and we do not serve a dead deity but a living God.

Our Jesus actually requires that we retire from our religious works. Check this out.

In Matthew 11:28, Jesus said, *"Are you tired? Worn out? Burned out on religion? Come to me. Get away with me and you will recover your life. I'll show you how to take a real rest. Walk with me, work with me, watch how I do it. Learn the unforced rhythms of grace. I won't lay anything heavy or ill-fitting on you. Keep company with me and you'll learn to live light and free."*

Through this incredible passage of scripture, Jesus is calling us to rest, to retire from our religious work. However, notice that Jesus doesn't want us to retire from all work. He instead invites us to work with him as friends, not for him as slaves.

Righteousness is exactly that! Right standing with God and retirement from the work that other religions require to receive relationship with God.

The good news is that Jesus does all the work and we receive the reward.

Let's talk about retirement for a moment. I don't know about you, but for me, Thanksgiving actually provides the perfect picture of retirement. Ideally, Thanksgiving is a holiday where we rest from our work and spend the day enjoying family, friends, fun, food, and a tryptophan-filled nap.

Now, minus the turkey coma, many people have a retirement plan in place to make the Thanksgiving holiday experience a lifelong reality. They work hard for thirty years to pay their bills, receive a pension, fill a retirement fund, and delete all debts. Spiritually speaking, this is exactly what Jesus accomplished for us on the cross. Jesus paid all of our bills, purchased our pension plan, filled our retirement fund, and deleted all of our debts. Now, according to Romans 13:8, "Our only debt is to love one another."

All Thanksgiving to Jesus, his work qualifies us to retire and receive a heavenly inheritance, an inheritance that, according to 1 Peter 1:5, "will never perish, spoil, or fade," and is kept in heaven for us protected by the power of God.

That means no stock market crash, no housing bubble, no depression, or economic downturn can destroy what Jesus worked so hard for us to receive.

So, if we are retired, in a spiritual sense, no longer required to work for our salvation, how should we spend our retirement?

Some choose to simply enjoy life by sitting around relaxing, shopping, vacationing, watching TV, and playing golf. Others restlessly wrestle with retirement, feeling complacent and purposeless. While many more discover that retirement is when the real work starts. When finally free from the requirement to work, people often find passion projects to fill their time, work that is more fun, fulfilling, and purposeful.

It is through these passion projects where people pour out their blood, sweat, and tears because they want to, not because they have to.

Sounds a lot like Jesus if you ask me.

Jesus did not have to leave his home in heaven to embrace the fallen, cursed conditions of our world. He didn't have to work back-breaking labor as a carpenter or wander around like a homeless man to pursue people with God's love, power, and the gospel message; but he did.

Jesus labored in love, not obligation.

His blood, sweat, and tears were poured out to pursue his passion project, us.

"For you know the grace of our Lord Jesus, that though he was rich, for your sake he became poor, so that through his poverty, we might become rich" (2 Cor. 8:9).

Why does this verse say "might"?

Because the offer is on the table, but it's our responsibility to receive it.

Jesus came to enrich us with the following:

- Retirement
- Righteousness
- Eternal rewards
- Heavenly Inheritance
- Relationship with God
- Redemption from slavery
- Restoration from sin
- The Holy Spirit

But you have to embrace it, receive it, trust him for it in faith. And when you do, God promises us adoption as his sons and daughters.

Through faith, we are adopted into the Father's family (Rom. 8:14–19; Gal. 4:5–7; Eph. 1:5; 1 John 3:1). Then and only then do we receive our explosive inheritance as we have been talking about.

Family Affair

Being a part of a family means having a certain level of responsibility. In my wife, Alissa's family, Thanksgiving is a production. Everything from the food to the décor looks like it belongs on the cover of a magazine or in a Hallmark movie.

It's a beautiful sight, but it doesn't happen unless every person in the family participates. In other words, Thanksgiving is family business, not a spectator sport. Every person is an important and integral part of the process. We all have a responsibility to contribute to the overall success of the meal, and when all is said and done, we are able to enjoy the fruit—rather, the turkey—of our labor. And it brings a sense of unity, satisfaction, and joy knowing that we accomplished this as a family.

There is a certain level of responsibility in every family. And in God's family, there is no exception. Jesus made us responsible to make disciples.

Jesus on the Numbers

According to the most recent count from the US census bureau, there are currently 7.4 billion people in the world today—7.4 billion! Don't let this number discourage you though, Jesus made the task of making disciples of all nations totally attainable.

If just one person, made one disciple every year, and taught that disciple to do the same, at the end of year 1, there would be two disciples, you and your original disciple. At the end of year 2, there would be four disciples: you, your original disciple, their disciple for the next year, and your new disciple for the next year. This pattern continues year after year until year 33, when 8.5 billion people would be discipled.

I don't think it's a coincidence that in thirty-three years, the amount of time Jesus lived on this earth, in thirty-three years, the entire world would be a part of God's family. Seems like a divine plan if you ask me.

It is also reported that 2.3 billion people claim to be Christian in the world today. If every single Christ follower did the one thing Christians are commissioned to do, the entire world would have a relationship with Jesus in three years. Jesus was only in ministry for three years. Again, not a coincidence.

So if this is the main thing we were called to do, how do we fulfill the Great Commission and make disciples?

The Good News is Jesus never asks us to do anything he hasn't already done himself.

Looking at his life, we see that Jesus invited people to follow him as he finished his Father's work. And Jesus did not only pursue the elite or pursue the people he would most enjoy living life with, no. Jesus called Peter, who would question every move Jesus made.

He called a pessimistic doubter named Thomas, a despised tax collector named Matthew, a fanatical Jew named Simon the zealot, a thief and betrayer named Judas, and a whole gang of unschooled, unpolished, unpopular fishermen.

Hashtag squad.

This was Jesus's posse, his people, his clique. And Jesus was ride or die for his disciples and eventually chose death on a cross to ensure that he could spend eternity with the people he loved.

Jesus lived his life openly and transparently with these people. He taught, demonstrated, and empowered his followers. He modeled a kingdom lifestyle for his disciples and constantly gave grace as his followers failed and fell from time to time.

This is our model.

Like Jesus, we are called to extend an invitation to others that says, "Follow me as I follow Christ" (1 Cor. 11:1). Once someone accepts that invitation, allow your life to be visible and accessible to them. Show disciples how to love by the way we love them and others around them. Allow our failures and faults to comfort those following us because we won't always get this discipleship thing right. We are all in process and discipleship includes owning our sin and modeling confession as well.

Anyone can do this.

Paul wrote to his disciple Timothy, saying, "Don't let anyone look down on you for your youth, but instead, set an example in your speech, conduct, love, faith, and purity" (1 Tim. 4:12).

This wasn't an age thing, but a spiritual maturity thing. There is always someone with less faith, understanding, and spiritual maturity than us. Anyone following Jesus can make disciples.

It's the spirit of pride that says, "I can't make disciples." You can! How do I know this? Jesus not only gave us this great responsibility, but he also gave us the "response ability."

Jesus is our model, and he made disciples perfectly. Since Jesus literally lives in every believer through his Spirit, that means the ability to respond to the Great Commission by making disciples like Jesus did dwells in us too. Again, through the Holy Spirit, Jesus has given us "response ability." It's his power at work that makes this work.

Ask Jesus to make disciples through you, and he will. Put the focus on the Christ in you and not you alone. Place your faith in his perfection, power, presence, and sufficiency. That's how disciples are made.

Paul encouraged the Christians in Rome when he wrote, "I myself am convinced, my brothers and sisters, that you yourselves are full of goodness, filled with knowledge, and competent to instruct one another" (Rom. 5:14).

You don't need to be a biblical scholar, theologian, or understand every doctrine in scripture to disciple. Can you read? That's really all you need. Start in the book of John, Romans, or Ephesians. Read the scriptures together, pray together, serve together, eat and enjoy life together. This is how Jesus made disciples.

One of the greatest joys in my life, other than marrying Alissa, has been discipling a student named Joel. We met more than seven years ago at church when I was a life group leader for his freshmen class. Outside of our weekly life group meetings, Joel and I met for lunch, watched sports, went skateboarding, played games, and talked about everything from faith and girls to aliens and dinosaurs. And over time, Joel became part of our family. Alissa and I love Joel, and we all do life together.

Joel is now leading at his church, discipling other students, and passionately preaching the gospel on his college campus.

We all need to be on the giving and receiving end of discipleship. Even pastors have people mentoring them. Discipleship cycles. Iron sharpening iron. We need each other.

If mentorship sounds appealing, ask God and he will gladly give you one.

When Alissa and I finally found our church home, I started praying for godly mentorship and God brought a pastor named Ken into my life. We started meeting in the mornings on a monthly basis to talk faith, marriage, work, life, and anything else that came up. Pastor Ken would also courageously try converting me into a coffee drinker, which still hasn't happened, but Ken has added great value to my life and faith. I value Ken and thank God for the accountability, encouragement, and prayer that I receive from that discipleship relationship.

Treasures in Heaven

Through a discipleship relationship in my life, I was recently challenged to change how I think about "storing up treasure in heaven." This is a reference from Matthew 6:19–21 where Jesus taught that our hearts will be invested wherever we invest our treasures.

Before this conversation, I selfishly thought that I was storing up wealth for myself in heaven through my good deeds and religious works. I thought that I could earn things from God through spiritual disciplines like fasting, prayer, meditation, giving, and even discipling others.

It was a loving challenge, but the confrontation cut deep into my heart. I was asked,

"What are the treasures of heaven?"

I had never really thought about this before.

When reading the description of heaven from the book of Revelation, we discover that the things we value here on earth like gold, silver, rubies, pearls, and other precious stones are simply the common décor of heaven. God literally walks on streets made of gold.

If the things we value on earth, aren't valued in heaven, what are the treasures of heaven?

Think about this.

On our death beds, we will not care about our accumulated riches, instead we will crave our relationships, our family and friends.

The real treasure of heaven is found in the people that Jesus purchased with his own blood. Our Father literally bankrupted heaven and poured out his most precious resource to purchase people. God's treasury is full of his family and friends.

Relationships are the real riches and making disciples stores up diamonds for our Father in heaven.

So our job, our Great Commission, is to find treasure among the trash, to take coal and make diamonds through the heat and pressure of living life together in discipleship relationships. We want to make diamonds who will shine for our Heavenly Father and show off his radiance, brilliance, and beauty. To help people discover their identities as sons and daughters of the king. The goal of discipleship is to help others become fully devoted followers of Jesus in every area of their lives, and by doing so, we store treasure in heaven.

This idea should radically change the way we view people and our purpose here on earth. Discipleship isn't always easy. These relationships, like diamonds, do not form overnight. They require trust and time to be built. It happens over daily displays of care and concern. It's an investment of time and money and can be costly, but I guarantee you, discipleship will be the greatest investment you ever make. At the very least, it's a wise investment. The book of wisdom, Proverbs tells us, "He who wins souls is wise" (Prov. 11:30).

We are employed and equipped with this specific purpose in mind, to make disciples. And in our time together, we have discovered that our inheritance in the Holy Spirit was intended to provide the power tools to destroy the works of the devil and build the church. Instead of a hammer, God handed us a nail gun. Instead of a pickaxe, he provided a pack of C4. Instead of a screwdriver, God gave us a drill gun. We have been given godly power tools for the task of tearing down demonic strongholds and building up godly temples.

Yes, I said temples.

We the church, the body of Christ, the royal priesthood, are filled and inhabited by the Holy Spirit as a temple, as the dwelling place of God. Not only that, we carry his glory wherever we go. And that's what we are called to do, go!

Go and share the gospel. Go and make disciples. Go!

But don't just go, give!

When Jesus sent out his disciples with the dunamis power of God, he said, "Freely you have received, freely give" (Matt. 10:8). Our inheritance was not meant to hoard, but to hand out! When it comes to our inheritance, the only saving plan we should be pursuing is the salvation of souls. If you have never read the parable of the talents (Matt. 25:14–30), right now is a good time. Jesus did not give us time, talents, tools, and treasure as an inheritance to simply store until he returns. Jesus expects us to work and invest our inheritance.

Did you know that God will keep us accountable for the investment of our inheritance? Jesus talks about an accountability judgment on several occasions. You can reference the parable of the talents above, the parable of the wise and faithful servants from Matthew 24:45–51, or the sheep and goat judgment from Matthew 25:31–46. If you think that's harsh, you don't yet understand what is at stake. We are talking about the eternal judgment of souls here: heaven or hell, forever.

Wouldn't it be just to judge someone who had the cure for cancer and kept it to themselves? That's what we're talking about. As Christ followers, we have the cure for the spiritual cancer of sin. Keeping the cure to ourselves is not an option. Jesus paid much too high a price for us to keep quiet.

Again, we do not work for our inheritance, we work with our inheritance. God, who does not want anyone to perish but for all people to repent (2 Pet. 3:9), has gifted us everything we need to reach the hurting and those far from him. So freely give what you have freely been given. Give the gospel and the power of God to anyone in need! Lives are literally at stake. That's not meant to be a guilt trip either. Instead, it should excite and awaken the inner superhero in us all!

For God so loved the world that he gave (John 3:16), and as Jesus said, "It is more blessed to give than to receive" (Acts 20:35). You have an inheritance, but the blessing comes from the investing.

As Christ followers, we are called, commissioned, and commanded to make disciples; to be fruitful and multiply. Our inheritance is for gifting, our gifting is for serving, and our salvation is for sharing.

ID Check

Friend, you are not normal. Like Neo from the Matrix, you are the chosen one. You are God's chosen vessel to spread the good news of what Jesus has done. You are the answer to poverty, injustice, war, famine, disease, addiction, human trafficking, crime, gang violence, and all other works of the devil.

Like Clark Kent, you may appear normal, but there is an *S* on your chest. The same power that created the universe is the same power that raised Christ from the dead, and that power resides in you through the Holy Spirit.

You are anything but normal. You are called by God! Called to follow Jesus, not to church, not to Bible study, not to Ed Flander's house. Called to follow Jesus like Bruce Wayne follows the Bat-Signal. Called to listen to the Holy Spirit as he highlights the places and people who need healing, rescue, encouragement, deliverance, and salvation. Called to reconcile people back to their Creator. Called to bring the walking dead back to life. Called to bring hope to the hopeless, purpose to the aimless, joy to the downcast, healing to the hurting, wholeness to the broken, justice to the oppressed, food to the hungry, clothing to the cold, and friendship to the lonely. You have inherited the answer to people's prayers. You have been called and chosen. You are a child of God. This is who you are and whose you are, so be godly.

You have godly power, and with great power comes great responsibility. So use that power to invest your inheritance in the kingdom of God. Jesus told us "where our treasure is, there our heart will be also" (Matt. 6:21). Invest in the kingdom of heaven. Be about your Father's business. Leave a legacy of leading people to the Lord and allowing them to experience the blessing of the Peter Parker Process.

You have the dunamis power through the Holy Spirit to transform and save this planet. One person at a time, we can make a difference. It's time that we take what Jesus paid for and invest our inheritance to see souls saved and our gracious God glorified.

The Final Exam

I want to end this book with a challenge, a capstone project if you will.

As you consider your inheritance and all that God has done, given, promised, and prepared for you, I want you to put this book down and pray.

Ask the Holy Spirit to give you a name, then pick up the phone and call or text that person.

Tell them about their inheritance.

Tell them that becoming a superhero is not a fantasy, but a biblical reality.

Tell them about the power of Jesus to rescue sinners who have been separated from the God who loves them.

Share the gospel, tell them your testimony. Invite them to leave their sin and follow Jesus.

Tell them about the Holy Spirit who empowers people to solve any problem, big or small, that resulted from the fall.

I challenge you to invest your inheritance.

An adventure awaits the willing.

God bless.

Interested to read another awesome title from author Matthew Jones? Check out his first book, *From Mushrooms to the Messiah*.

From Mushrooms to the Messiah

How do you define success?

Is it a flourishing family life, prosperous career, healthy marriage, scholastic achievement, or physical fitness? Maybe your idea of success is a combination of the above. No matter how you define success, your journey to the top of that mountain requires commitment. *From Mushrooms to the Messiah* follows one man's journey to discover how to make and keep commitments that will ultimately provide the success and fulfillment that many of us desire.

Prepare yourself for a wild ride through fraternity life and into the drug abuse that brought one man face-to-face with the God who would turn his life upside down. No matter your religion or worldview, *From Mushrooms to the Messiah* will test your understanding of God and redefine faith while offering a timeless and unique love story the world has never known. What are you waiting for? An adventure awaits the willing.

From Mushrooms to the Messiah can be found wherever books are sold, including Amazon, Barnes and Nobles, Kindle, and more.

ABOUT THE AUTHOR

Matthew Jones is the senior associate pastor at Harvest Valley Church in Pleasanton, California, along with his wife Alissa. Together, they live in Livermore, California, with their one-year-old daughter Ellie and are currently awaiting the birth of their son Judah. Matthew and Alissa are passionate about raising up the next generation of Jesus followers while equipping and revitalizing the Church. Matthew and Alissa also look forward to growing their family and the kingdom of God. Besides pastoral ministry, Matthew is the international program manager at Berkeley City College, the author of the autobiographical adventure, *From Mushrooms to the Messiah*, and holds a master's degree in psychology. For more information about Matthew Jones, please visit his Instagram or Facebook profiles @ JonesN4Jesus.

CPSIA information can be obtained
at www.ICGtesting.com
Printed in the USA
LVHW010314200721
693160LV00007B/1074